How to Organize and Direct
the Church Choir

How to Organize and Direct the Church Choir

by

Dayton W. Nordin

Parker Publishing Company, Inc.

West Nyack, New York

Library of Congress Cataloging in Publication Data

Nordin, Dayton W
  How to organize and direct the church choir.

  1. Church music. 2. Choirs (Music) 3. Conducting,
Choral. I. Title.
MT88.N74   783.8   73-302
ISBN 0-13-425207-1

How This Book Will Benefit You

This book tells how to plan, organize, manage, and direct a successful church music program. Its intent is entirely practical: to help you achieve the best possible results with the choral and instrumental resources available to your church. In form, the book follows the music-making process step-by-step, from initial planning through the presentation in the worship service.

Chapter 1 tells how to plan your church music program, keeping it flexible, dynamic, and responsive to the needs of parish worship today.

Chapter 2 considers the business side of church music and offers specific methods for building a smooth-working church music department.

Chapter 3 discusses various kinds of church choirs, and gives directions for designing a choir specifically suited to your kind of church, your kind of worship services, and your kind of music. It tells how to recruit singers and instrumental players, and how to maintain the high percentage of attendance which is so vital to your success.

Chapter 4 considers the facilities for music which are found in church buildings, and how these may best be used. The physical and acoustical properties of the choir loft and rehearsal room exert an enormous influence on the sound of music as performed in church, an influence which directors too frequently ignore or underestimate.

Chapter 5 proposes practical tests which can help you determine in advance what music will be effective with your choir, and appropriate to your worship services.

Chapter 6 shows how to use total programming in church music, coordinating choir music, congregational hymns and responses, organ, and instrumental music into a cohesive unit.

Chapter 7 emphasizes the importance of your total mastery of each score, as distinct from your general knowledge of music. It proposes a time-tested method of score study which will increase the effectiveness of your choral conducting.

Chapter 8 tells how to plan and conduct the church choir rehearsal as a stimulating musical experience for the singers, not merely as preparation for public performance. It also suggests time-saving methods of teaching music to amateur singers.

Chapter 9 shows how to organize and produce special musical events in your church, or away from church: concerts, oratorios, cantatas, hymn and choir festivals, broadcasts, and recordings.

Chapter 10 considers the presentation of music as an important part of congregational worship; how to make sure that your choir says something worthwhile every Sunday.

Volunteer church choirs are an integral part of the musical, religious, and cultural life of nearly every community in our land. The success of such choirs depends largely upon the skill and energy of their directors. Working with volunteer singers is always a challenge, and it can be a deeply gratifying musical adventure. But it can also be a frustrating and unhappy experience if the director is not able to cope with the peculiar and recurrent problems which arise from working with singers of widely varying ages and musical abilities.

I had originally intended a career in public school music, but for more than four decades have found musical satisfaction and spiritual joy in church music. This book was written to encourage and assist school music teachers and others who ought to employ their talents in this important Christian service.

Dayton W. Nordin

Table of Contents

Part I: How to Organize the Church Choir

Assessing the Present Program (19) Church Music Is Dynamic, not Static (19) Church Choirs Exist to Lead and Inspire (20) Congregational Personality Shapes the Music Program (20) Differing Modes of Worship Require Differing Forms of Music (21) Status and Support of the Choir (22) Church Choir: Essential or Peripheral? (22) In Worship, Music Is Subordinate (22) Music Within the Total Program of the Church (23) Objectives and Priorities of the Church Administration (23) What Changes, if Any, Are Desired? (23) Music for Worship, Evangelism, Education, Sociality, Prestige (24) To Win Support, Consider the Needs of Others (24) Musical Resources and Worship Requirements (26) Adapting the Program to Fit the Musical Resources (26) SATB: The Basic Church Choir (27) The Unison Children's Choir (28) Providing Music for Multiple Services (28) Choir Membership: Inclusive or Exclusive? (28) Professionals in the Church Choir (29) Using Instruments in the Worship Service (29) Establishing the "Official" Church Music Program (30)

Introduction: Doing Means More Than Knowing (31) Organize Yourself First (31) Saving More Time for the Music (31) A Place to Work (32) A Time to Work (33) A Way to Work (33) Finances: Income and Expense (34) The Wise Director Handles No Cash (34) Follow Standard Purchasing Procedures (34) Making a Budget Forecast (35) Keeping Records: More Facts Faster (35) Correct Decisions Depend on Accurate Information (35) Professional or

Organizing the Church Music Department (*cont.*)

3. Building and Maintaining an Adequate Choir . . . .

Building and Maintaining an Adequate Choir (*cont.*)

4. Improving Facilities for Church Music . . . .

Improving Facilities for Church Music (*cont.*)

Harpsichords: Delightful but Delicate (94) Electronic Instruments: Past, Present, Future (95)

Your Program Is No Better Than Your Choice of Music (98) Music Affects Every Performer and Listener (98) To Be Truly Beautiful, Music Must Be Appropriate (99) Unsuitable Music Is the Root of Many Choir Problems (100) Church Music as a Special Form of Religious Music (100) Music, by Nature, Is Neither Sacred nor Christian (100) Religious Music vs. Church Music (101) Great Church Music: God-Expressive and Economical (102) Look for Beauty, Emotion, Simplicity, Strength, Integrity, Originality (102) Great Church Music Brings an Ageless Message (103) Authoritarian Standards for Church Music (103) Introducing New Musical Idioms in the Worship Service (104) Jazz, Folk, and Contemporary Music in Church (105) Essentials: Great Text, Expressive Music, Practicality (106) Singing Something of Significance (106) In the Beginning . . . The Word (106) Text Is the Distinctive Feature of Song (106) Every Distinguished Text Is a Drama in Miniature (107) Expressing Christian Thought in Noble Language (107) Problem Texts: Translations, Archaisms, Redundance (107) Testing a Text by Reading Aloud (108) Unfair to Pre-Empt Congregational Hymns for Choir Use (109) Music Should Give Wings to the Words (109) Music and Text: Each Should Strengthen the Other (109) Skilled Composers Use Varied Choral Styles (110) Fetishism and Prejudice in Church Music (110) Is Instrumental Accompaniment Really Necessary? (111) Additional Instruments Increase Interest and Impact (111) The Best Music Is the Music That Best Fits Your Choir (112) Intentions, Pretensions, and Realities (112) Building a Repertory of Enduring Value (113) How and Where to Find Suitable Church Music (113) Expect one in 100 to Be Right for You (113) Music Discoveries Are Unpredictable (113) Scanning Music Dealers' Collections (114) Music for the Children's Choir (114)

Part II: How to Direct the Church Choir

Programming Is Professional (118) Programming: Key to Control (118) "Success" Is Fulfilling One's Potential (118) The Director Cannot Escape Responsibility for Poor Performance (119) Counting

Programming Music for Superior Performance (*cont.*)

Interpreting Choral Scores (*cont.*)

How to Organize and Direct
the Church Choir

Part I

How to Organize the
Church Choir

1 Planning a Practical Church Music Program

ASSESSING THE PRESENT PROGRAM

Church Music Is Dynamic, not Static

From the beginning, song has been the voice of Christian worship.

"Speak to one another in the words of Psalms, hymns, and spiritual songs," wrote the Apostle Paul to his followers at Ephesus. "Sing hymns and Psalms to the Lord, with praise in your hearts." (Ephesians 5:9)

For nearly 20 centuries, Christians at worship have used music in church precisely as Paul suggested: to speak to each other; to express praise to the Lord.

But while the objectives and purposes of church music have not changed, the forms of church music have changed dramatically, and are changing still. Change may seem to come slowly in one's lifetime. But in the perspective of a generation or a century, changes are enormous. Contrast the Lutheran liturgical service of J.S. Bach's day with present-day services.

Then	Now
Worship began at 7:00 a.m., lasting 4 hours.	Worship lasts about 60 minutes.
Sermon: 1½ to 2 hours	Sermon: 15-20 minutes
Hymns: 30-40 stanzas	Hymns: 3-5 stanzas
Choir: Cantata, 20-40 minutes	Choir: Anthem, 2-4 minutes

Worship practices reflect the lifestyle of the congregation, and this is never static—

• Neighborhoods and communities change.

- Congregations grow older, or sometimes younger.
- Church administration and pastor may change.
- Musical tastes and fashions change.
- Musical resources and abilities change.

The church music program that does not faithfully reflect the changes that take place in the congregation is in constant danger of becoming obsolete, irrelevant, or inadequate. Those who plan and administer the music of the church should periodically review the current program to make certain that it is fulfilling its primary functions:

- To help all people speak to each other.
- To help all people express their praise to the Lord.

Church Choirs Exist to Lead and Inspire

Nowhere in the New Testament is the use of choirs suggested for Christian worship. Yet organized bands of singers are to be found in churches throughout Christendom because choirs serve two practical functions in corporate worship:

- The choir leads the congregation in worship ritual.
- The choir brings into the service great spiritual ideas expressed in song.

Congregational Personality Shapes the Music Program

The personality of the congregation will determine the kind of music program the church will support, and the type of music that will be effective in its worship services. This corporate personality is formed by the interaction of several factors.

Denominational Affiliation. Each church group, whether Roman Catholic, Presbyterian, or Amish, retains certain historic religious practices which it feels are distinctive and important.

Cultural Heritage. The ancestors of Americans came from many continents. Worship customs and traditions of the country of national origin persist for several generations, sometimes to a marked degree. Greek and Armenian immigrants brought to America Christian traditions which differ greatly from those brought by the Irish or German Christians.

Social Environment. The social concerns and outlook of a congregation strongly influence its character. The personality of an inner-city congregation will differ markedly from that of a congregation in a suburb or small town.

Economic Status. The income level and property holdings of church members have a significant effect on congregational personality. A view of the world from the top of the economic heap differs greatly from a view from the bottom.

The director of music in any church should strive to provide "good" music, but, in addition to being "good," it must also be "right" for that congregation. A high Episcopal church in a wealthy all-white suburb may find its ideal of church music in a boy choir and an austere repertory of Tallis, Byrd, Wesley, and Walmisley. But on the other side of the street, the Federated church may delight in its teen-aged choir exuberantly belting out folk-type gospel songs to the twang of electric guitar and tintinnabulation of tambourine. As different as such choirs may be from each other, each may be exactly right in its time and place.

The important thing is that there be a mutual respect and compatibility among director, clergy, congregation, and choir. The director should genuinely enjoy the kinds of choirs and the type of music that the congregation enjoys. The congregation's musical horizon should be continually extended. But the director should remember that an attempt at instant and radical reform in the views and tastes of a congregation may result in severe cultural shock.

If a director cannot, with good artistic conscience, provide the type of music that is both "good and right" for his congregation, he should move on. In church music, as elsewhere, no one wins disputes about matters of taste.

Differing Modes of Worship Require Differing Forms of Music

There is no one kind of church music that is "right" for all churches and all occasions. The kind of music that is "right" or appropriate depends upon the mode of worship used in the church. In some congregations, this mode is highly ecclesiastical, in the literal sense of being "called away" or separated from the ordinary (secular) world. In such churches, a clear distinction is drawn between that which is sacred and that which is secular. Withdrawn from the world, the ecclesiastical church uses an archaic language, distinctive vestment for participants in the service, imitative architecture and decor, and traditional musical idioms.

Other congregations try deliberately to dissolve barriers between the sacred and the secular. They wish to identify very closely with contemporary, everyday life. In such churches, clergy wear normal business suits. Vernacular language is used. The church building differs little from other public auditoriums. The church music sounds almost identical with current secular music.

Modes of worship are neither rigid nor static. At times, a congregation or a denomination will sense a need for change. Thus, the Roman Catholic church in the 1960's replaced its traditional Latin mass and modal psalmtones with local vernaculars and popular musical idioms. In the 1970's, the Greek Orthodox church broke with centuries of tradition and began to permit the use of local language in its liturgy.

The prevailing mode of worship in any congregation is normally established by the pastor, following denominational guidelines. Because music is one of the most practical and effective means of expressing change in the church, the director of music must remain keenly sensitive and responsive to changing modes of worship.

STATUS AND SUPPORT OF THE CHOIR

Church Choir: Essential or Peripheral?

The status of the choir and its support by the congregation varies widely from church to church, and generally reflects the worship traditions of the congregation. In churches which use a formal mass or worship ritual, the leadership of a well-prepared choir has been found most helpful to the congregation. In such liturgical churches, the choir may be considered an integral part of worship.

Among other Protestant churches, the role of the choir may be less well defined. At one extreme is the congregation with a multiple-choir program of such magnitude that each church service takes on the aspect of a music festival, with a spectacular array of vested choirs of all types and ages. At the other extreme is the church where music may be relegated to the same peripheral status as the men's bowling league; choir is just another "church activity."

The healthy church music program is fluid and dynamic; it is capable of adaptation and change. The alert and energetic director will wish to expand the role of music in the worship services to the practical limit. But the ultimate role of music in worship is set by the pastor and church administration, not by the director. Aggressive expansion of musical activities without approval of the church leadership will almost certainly provoke controversy and resistance.

In Worship, Music Is Subordinate

The primary business of the Christian church is the worship of God. In worship, music plays a supporting role; music is "the hand-maid of religion."

The church choir is not a concert choir devoted to "art for art's sake." The music sung by the choir is not an end in itself, but has significance only because it is part of the worship of God.

In keeping with this subordinate status, the music department of the church ought to function smoothly within the framework of the total church program. Church choirs are not autonomous organizations, free to pursue independent ends and purposes. The church choir is basically a small part of the congregation which has assumed special musical responsibilities in the worship service. The director of music is employed to give choir members professional assistance to this end.

Music Within the Total Program of the Church

Granting that music is subordinate to worship, to what else in the total church program is it subordinate? Is music more or less important than church school, social service programs, or missions? The director is seldom able to change the relative status of music in the total church program, but it is important that he understand what that status is. A few questions may help to clarify the status of music in the church.

a. *What is permitted to compete or conflict with musical activities?* Are church members urged to teach Sunday School rather than sing in the choir? Are church organizations permitted to schedule their activities on choir rehearsal nights?

b. *How is the music program financed?* Is the music budget part of the general expense of the church? Or are choirs self-supporting through dues and fund-raising projects?

c. *Who helps to recruit choir personnel?* Does the church administration help, or is this considered solely the music director's problem?

d. *What percentage of the church budget is spent on music?* Has this percentage increased or decreased over the past years? What are intentions for the future?

OBJECTIVES AND PRIORITIES OF THE CHURCH ADMINISTRATION

What Changes, if Any, Are Desired?

At least once each season, the director of music should meet with the pastor and music committee to review the church music program. It is essential that there be complete understanding and agreement about the purposes and methods of the music department. If either the pastor or the director is new, a review of the objectives and priorities desired by the church administration should be made at the earliest opportunity.

If changes in the program are desired, either by the director of music or by the administration, it is most important that everyone understand the reason for the proposed changes and have an opportunity to discuss these. Since the church music program can operate successfully only with the full cooperation of all interested parties, it is vital that a consensus be reached. Otherwise, the director may find himself working very hard to achieve goals which no one else regards as important. Or, even worse, he may fail to achieve goals which the pastor and music committee do consider important.

Music for Worship, Evangelism, Education, Sociality, Prestige

It is quite possible that the church administration may be interested, and vitally so, in objectives which lie beyond the choir's primary role in the worship service. These may include the following ulterior goals.

Evangelism, singing at street meetings or revival campaigns; programs at retirement centers, hospitals, or corrective institutions.

Education, using music to teach Christian theology. Hymns, especially, are important summaries of doctrine. Some pastors may wish the choir to feature music of the denominational heritage to help preserve a distinctive cultural tradition.

Sociality, keeping the young people of the church "interested" may be considered much more important than technical excellence in musical performance.

Prestige of the church in the community is enhanced by well-done special musical events. In some communities, the competition among congregations for favorable notice and prestige may be covert but nonetheless intense. In extremely competitive circumstances, the special programs may actually be more important to the aims of the administration than excellence in Sunday worship music.

Fortunately for the director, multiple goals for the church music program are not necessarily incompatible. But the wise director ought to understand exactly what is expected of his program.

To Win Support, Consider the Needs of Others

The successful church music director is a catalyst; his presence makes things happen. He is an entrepreneur, and the success of his musical projects depends largely upon his ability to enlist the loyal and dedicated effort of many people.

A good way to win cooperation and support is to include in the music program the features which others believe to be important. The interests of others may not be identical with yours, but they are important in their eyes. Others will generally support your program to the degree that the program appears to satisfy and gratify their own needs and ambitions.

Whose support is required for a successful church music program? What would each reasonably expect from the program?

Pastor. A music program cannot succeed fully without the support of the pastor. He is responsible for the conduct of the service. It is important to him that music in the service be performed decently. This includes all of the music, choral and instrumental. He expects well-prepared leadership in the worship service. He may occasionally request specific musical selections, which should receive top priority.

Not every pastor is musical. Not all will support an ambitious church music program. Some regard music as of very minor importance to the purposes of the church. Others look on music as a competitor for congregational attention and approval; a few are openly hostile towards a strong music program. The director ought to understand the pastor's attitude and plan his activities within the parameter which is acceptable to the pastor.

Music Committee. The duties and authority of the church music committee greatly vary from congregation to congregation. The director should learn who is on the committee, when it meets, and what it does. In general, he should keep the committee informed of music department needs, problems, plans, and progress. The committee does not make music, but it helps to make the conditions under which music is produced.

Neither pastor nor committee wishes to be drawn into personal vendettas in the music department. The director should himself try to resolve conflicts and clashes in his department. Only when this proves to be impossible should he refer matters to the music committee.

Basically, the music committee wants a sound program, good performances, and a trouble-free staff.

Accompanists. They are partners, not drudges. Treat them with respect and consideration at all times. Encourage organists to be creative in the playing of hymn and anthem accompaniments. Help them utilize and develop their musical skills and interests. Solicit suggestions and use whatever is practical.

Choir Members. Unless the music program provides what the singers feel is worthwhile, there will be no program. Most wish to sing good music and perform it well. They seek to use their talent in the service of the church. Many wish to grow in musical skill and knowledge.

For some singers, self-realization through solo work or small ensembles is especially important. Most respond to personal recognition and sincere appreciation; these are among the most powerful of human motivations. Many enjoy the social activities of a choir. Nearly all are moved by the mystical feeling of "oneness" that pervades a hard-working choir.

Instrumentalists. A chance to use their musical abilities in church is most welcomed by instrumental players. Some have the capacity for solo work and should be given this opportunity. Most greatly enjoy ensemble work and accompanying the chorus. The music program should afford frequent opportunities for instrumental participation.

Congregation. Above all else, the congregation desires good leadership and support in their part of the service, hymns, and choral responses. Most churchgoers appreciate beautiful music, beautifully performed. They expect a Christian message in the music and a Christian attitude in its performance.

The congregation does not want distractions from worship, nor vainglorious displays from choir or organ. They do not wish to be a captive audience for ill-prepared musical experiments.

MUSICAL RESOURCES AND WORSHIP REQUIREMENTS

Adapting the Program to Fit the Musical Resources

The musical resources and worship requirements of all congregations undergo continual change. The basic format of the church music program should be continuously reviewed and altered to fit existing circumstances as often as necessary.

- What are the needs of your congregation . . . *now?*
- What are the musical resources of your congregation . . . *now?*

The effective church music program must be geared to today's congregation, not yesterday's nor tomorrow's. The director should plan as much program as the administration and congregation will support; certainly no more, hopefully no less. An effective program is custom-designed to utilize the full musical abilities within the congregation. There should be a place for every musical person who truly wishes to participate. No sincerely offered talent should be turned away.

It has been an all-too-common practice in church music to set up some stereotyped music program and then recruit only those who fit readily into it. A better program will result if the director would first inventory the vocal and instrumental resources in the congregation, then devise a departmental structure providing a place for all available musical talent.

SATB: The Basic Church Choir

The adult SATB choir is usually the foundation of the church music program. The administration may desire other types of choirs for varied purposes (see page 24). But if there is a paramount justification for a church choir, it is to lead the singing in the worship service. Voice-to-voice leadership is demonstrably more effective than organ-to-voice leadership. In an adult congregation, such voice-to-voice leadership is best provided by adult voices (less effectively by children or youth). Thus, whenever possible, the establishment of a strong adult SATB choir should be the very first objective of the director of music.

If leadership in the worship service is primary, the second most important function of the church choir is the presentation of beautiful sacred music. In the matter of repertory, the SATB choir has a commanding advantage. It can draw upon a vast and varied treasure of music accumulated by the Christian family over the past 400 years or more. There is perhaps more really good music available to the SATB choir than to any other type of musical ensemble, whether choral or instrumental. Excellent music is available to SATB choirs of very modest size and ability, and to suit any occasion.

Those who advocate church choirs for children and youth emphasize their value as "education and participation." But education and participation are important for adults, too. Children and young people can usually participate in school musical activities if they wish to do so. But in many communities, church choirs offer the only opportunity for adults to sing and to continue their musical interest and growth.

The Unison Children's Choir

Next in musical importance is the children's unison choir for unchanged voices. A well-disciplined unison choir can add a uniquely beautiful dimension to the musical experience of the church.

A Great Literature. Unison music is pure melody. There is a unique literature of sacred song which can be most effectively sung by a unison choir: plainsong, melodic chorales, and psalm tunes; songs and arias of the great classic composers; folksong from the world around.

Unison Song Is Basic. Unison singing is the basis of all choral art. The most complex choral scores are merely combinations of many unison voice-lines. A unison choir seems a logical place to teach unison singing, the most essential of choral skills.

In some large congregations, there may be sufficient personnel and resources to support an intermediate choir for youth who are not mature enough to participate in the SATB choir. A separate choir for youth should be considered only if there is a genuine need for it and enough genuine enthusiasm to keep it going.

Providing Music for Multiple Services

Multiple worship services often put a severe strain on a congregation's volunteer musical resources. To provide adequate musical leadership at all services, it is sometimes necessary to augment the available volunteers with professional singers. Here are some possible combinations where music must be provided at two services each Sunday:

Minor Service	*Major Service*
Rotation of vocal or instrumental solos or small ensembles	SATB choir
Children's or youth choir	SATB choir
Part of large SATB choir assigned to sing	Balance of large SATB choir
Professional choir	Same professional choir
Small, separate SATB choir	Large SATB choir
Professional quartette	SATB choir, including the professional quartette

Choir Membership: Inclusive or Exclusive?

In most churches, choir membership is based on two considerations: church affiliation and musical competence.

Church Affiliation. Some churches require that all choristers be bona fide members of the congregation. Others actively recruit students or townspeople, regardless of church membership.

Musical Competence. In some choirs, the director is the sole judge of who is qualified to sing. In others, the administration insists that the choir be open to any member who wishes to participate, regardless of previous musical training or experience. It is perhaps easier for the director to work with fewer, better-qualified voices. But some excellent church choirs will welcome anyone who really wants to sing and is willing to attend rehearsals faithfully.

If the director feels that he is handicapped by choir membership rules, or the lack of them, he may find that these can be changed with no great difficulty.

Professionals in the Church Choir

Most church choristers are unpaid volunteers. But some large and affluent congregations supplement their volunteers with paid professionals. Sometimes only one or two voices are hired, mainly to bolster up weaker sections of the choir. Other churches employ a mixed quartette, whose members usually sing the solos in anthems, perform as a quartette, and lend professional leadership to each voice section. A very few churches employ an entirely professional choir.

The use of professionals quickly solves choir personnel problems. But it may in the long term be harmful to the overall church music program if it deters the director from developing the musical talent within his own congregation, or deprives capable volunteers of the opportunity for solo singing.

Using Instruments in the Worship Service

The tasteful use of instruments can greatly increase the effectiveness of choral music in church. The directors of professional groups, such as Robert Shaw, Roger Wagner, Norman Luboff, Gregg Smith, and Robert De Cormier, are especially skilled in the use of light instrumental support for their superb choirs. The director of the church choir can learn a great deal about the instrumental enhancement of choral sound by listening to their concerts and recordings.

Elaborate instrumental resources are not required for effective choral accompaniments. A single instrument, appropriately scored, can make the difference between a memorable performance and an ordinary one.

Of course, the instrumental players in the congregation need not be restricted to the playing of choir accompaniments. The possibilities for solos and ensembles are almost unlimited. A brass choir with organ and percussion offers exciting musical possibilities.[1] Instrumental music can be scheduled in the service wherever voluntaries are permitted: preludes, offertories, postludes. The more good instrumental music the director can include, the more interesting and attractive his total music program is likely to be.

ESTABLISHING THE "OFFICIAL" CHURCH MUSIC PROGRAM

The basic structure for the church music program should be determined before the choir season gets under way. If there are changes from the previous season, these should have been approved by the pastor and music committee. All should be in agreement on an "official" structure for the music program. This will assure that the financial resources and the musical energies of the congregation will be coordinated into the most constructive and effective channels.

In some situations, where there has been no officially sanctioned music program, the results have been chaotic. There are sometimes musical members of the congregation, who, for one reason or another, will refuse to cooperate in the regular church music program. Yet these may demand the right to perform in church, either as soloists or in groups. The structure of the program should be flexible enough to accommodate an occasional guitar-strumming folk singer, jazz combo, or pop-gospel group. But it is absolutely essential that these not be permitted to challenge or displace the established musical organizations, nor to drain membership from them. A faddist group or an alienated little clique working outside of the established program can ruin the church choir, but can never replace it.

---

[1] There are good examples on this recording: *Heroic Music for Organ, Brass, and Percussion*—Columbia MS 6354. E. Power Biggs is the organist.

2 Organizing the Church Music Department

INTRODUCTION: DOING MEANS MORE THAN KNOWING

Success in conducting a church choir demands both musical ability and organizational ability. Which ability is the more important?

Some experienced observers estimate that in church music, success depends about 90% on organizational ability and about 10% on musical ability! Musical ability is obviously indispensable, but in church music, at least, no amount of musical knowledge can overcome the lack of organizational skill. "Failure" in church music most frequently connotes a "failure to organize."

"To organize" means to put things together so that they will work effectively. In basic terms, organizing a church music program means to assess the musical abilities within the congregation and channel these into effective use in the worship service.

ORGANIZE YOURSELF FIRST

Saving More Time for the Music

The first thing the director should organize is himself. It is particularly important for the part-time church music director to do this. Few of us have unlimited amounts of time to devote to our church music. Efficient personal organization will insure that whatever time can be set aside for church music will be invested to the best possible musical advantage.

Good personal organization implies a place to work, a time to work, and a way to work.

A Place to Work

It is practical and convenient to operate from two bases: one at home, one at church. The link between the two bases is an attaché case (briefcase or dispatch case) containing all currently useful church music materials. This case should be used for absolutely no other purpose.

The home base is the Center for Research, Planning, and Development. It should be equipped for these functions with a keyboard instrument, work desk, reference books, typewriter, and adequate filing facilities. The latter is of special importance; an orderly and well-organized filing system is at the very heart of the organizational process.

The filing system should accommodate:

a. The director's special copy of each anthem in the church choir library.
b. Copies of new anthems and other music for study, reference, and possible purchase.
c. Past records pertaining to the church music program: music schedules of previous seasons, service bulletins, attendance records, etc.

A four-drawer, legal-size filing cabinet will usually suffice.

The director's base at church is the Production Supervisor's Office. It should be in or near the choir's workshop (rehearsal room) where the music is to be assembled for use. This production office need not be elaborate, but should afford a quiet corner for conferences, and desk space.

The special attaché case should provide separate compartments for:

a. The director's copy of each anthem currently in rehearsal.
b. Choir attendance records.
c. The rehearsal outline or schedule.
d. Correspondence and other material relating to current special programs or musical projects.

If the director keeps these important items in this attaché case at all times, and in no other place—ever—he will save himself a great deal of time and irritation. In departing for the choir rehearsal, he need remember only one item—the attaché case—for everything that he will need at rehearsal should be in it.

A Time to Work

Experienced teachers of music agree that pupils make the best progress with regular daily practice. Directors of church music make the best progress in exactly the same way: *regular daily practice.* The choral director, no matter how skilled or experienced, is a student of music, and should remain so all of his life. There is always something more to learn.

At the very least, the director should expect to spend one hour each day on his homework. This homework is more likely to be done regularly if one specific hour of each day is set aside for the purpose. During this study hour, the director should work at whatever will help the choir most in the immediate future:

- Re-study scores that are troublesome during rehearsal.
- Analyze attendance records.
- Follow up the absentees.
- Contact prospective new choir members.
- Review new choral publications.
- Schedule music for the next unit.
- Outline the next rehearsal.
- Write music notes for the church bulletin.
- Research the background of music in rehearsal.
- Study periodicals or books on church music.
- Listen to choral recordings.
- Plan improvements in church music facilities.
- Devise ways to make church music more interesting.

One hour a day may not be sufficient for all that needs to be done, but at least it will be a start.

A Way to Work

The successful director, though he is primarily a musician, uses the techniques of business administration in the management of the church music department:

- *He makes decisions,* basing these on fact, not on hopes and wishes.
- *He takes action,* communicating his decisions clearly, in writing.
- *He knows his goals,* and keeps things moving towards these objectives.

- *He delegates responsibility*, making fullest use of the talent and ability of others. He gives others a chance to express themselves and develop their own abilities.
- *He supervises progress*, objectively assessing the progress of all music in rehearsal to insure adequate preparation on schedule.
- *He remembers to say "thanks,"* being certain that there are no "thankless jobs" nor "forgotten men" in his music program.

FINANCES: INCOME AND EXPENSE

The Wise Director Handles No Cash

It takes money to operate the church music department. Some choirs are independently self-supporting; others are maintained as part of the general expense of the congregation.

The source of financing should be of no concern to the director; raising money should not be his responsibility in any case. But inevitably, he will be involved in the spending of money for music and supplies, for soloists, for equipment and repairs, for improvements and maintenance.

Avoid handling any actual cash for the music department. Collecting and disbursing money is the function of a treasurer, whether a choir treasurer or church treasurer. These people tend, by nature, to be careful and systematic beings. Each follows an orderly and usually logical procedure for doing his work. Find out what these procedures are and follow them meticulously. These are safeguards and assurances for the good of all who must handle someone else's money.

Follow Standard Purchasing Procedures

Purchases for the music department should always be transactions between the church and the supplier; the director should never become a middle-man.

If purchase orders are requested or required by church policy, use them.

Have all merchandise shipped to the church; never to your home address.

Have all charges billed directly to the church; never to your own account for later reimbursement.

Verify all invoices as soon as presented, and, if correct, see that they are passed along promptly for payment. Delay on your part may jeopardize the credit of the church.

Making a Budget Forecast

Most churches operate on a budget. The general budget of the congregation is the sum of various departmental budgets. Each department of the church, including music, may be asked to prepare a forecast for each fiscal year.

The music budget should be prepared in consultation by the music committee and director of music. This will give the director an opportunity to see that the needs of his department receive consideration in the general budget.

Budget estimates are generally of two kinds, operating expense and capital expense.

Operating Expense. This is the money needed for current salaries and services to keep the department running: director, accompanist, soloists, maintaining the organ, tuning pianos, cleaning robes, etc.

Capital Expense. Money spent for equipment and materials of long-term usefulness: new music, musical instruments, robes, improvements to the rehearsal room, audio equipment, etc.

Budget requests should be supported with specific cost estimates. The director should also indicate a priority among his requested budget items. Tuning the organ may be more important than a new tape deck for the stereo. New music may be more important than new robes.

KEEPING RECORDS: MORE FACTS FASTER

Correct Decisions Depend on Accurate Information

The administrator of a church music department is continually making decisions. His decisions are more likely to be correct if they are based on fact as opposed to intuition, emotion, or plain guesswork. Problems can rarely be solved unless underlying causes are clearly understood. Snap judgement often results in costly blunders.

The facts upon which to base decisions are most readily available in a good records-keeping system. The key to the most puzzling and persistent problems may often be found there.

The records system should cover two major areas in the church music program: personnel and music.

Personnel records include information about the musicians, their talents, interests, training, and experience. A detailed record of attendance should be kept for each individual, each voice section, and each choir.

Music records include schedules of music to be performed and an analytic record of past performances of each anthem.

Professional or Dilettante? Records Tell the Difference

Nothing more surely separates the dilettante director from the real professional than the systematic keeping of vital records. Perhaps most musicians dislike "bookkeeping chores," the professional no less than the amateur. But the professional keeps records because he realizes that his records system is the nerve-center of the entire church music program. Written plans are the best means of coordinating the varied musical activities in the church. The records system provides the only practical means of monitoring and controlling departmental projects.

It takes some time to set up and maintain a good records system. But the time invested in this pays immense dividends in musical results. Overall, efficient records systems are not time-consuming, they are time-saving.

For some kinds of records, such as attendance, printed forms are convenient, and are available at small cost. But a suitable records system can be set up at practically no expense with such simple materials as index cards, file folders, and plain sheets of paper.

Here is a summary of useful kinds of church choir records:

Personnel Records

> Individual singer's registration card.
> Attendance chart, for rehearsals and services.
> Recruiting file; persons interested but not active in church choir.
> Instrumental players; all types, all instruments.
> Professional soloists, available for special programs.

Music Records

> Choral music scheduled for performance.
> Production memos; special resources required for an anthem.
> Hymn schedule.
> Weekly rehearsal plan.
> Performance register; record of past performance of each anthem.

Church bulletin archive, with marginal notes.

Special program packet; information on each past major musical project.

ACCOMPANISTS AS PART OF THE LEADERSHIP TEAM

Developing Team Leadership

The director should be alert to the possibility of jurisdictional and ideological struggles among directors and accompanists on his music staff. Dissension is not unknown among church musicians, and nothing more quickly undermines the effectiveness of the leadership team. Much conflict can be avoided if everyone's place on the team is clearly defined by the church administration at the time of hiring. But Christian forbearance is always needed to prevent small differences of opinion from flaring into open antagonism. Tolerance comes more easily if all members of the leadership team are truly dedicated to the cause of church music. Each must at times subordinate his personal feelings and opinions for the sake of a smooth and successful performance of the music.

But even in the best of circumstances, the administrator of a church music department should, like Solomon, pray for an understanding heart (1 Kings 3:9).

The Church Organist: Star Soloist or Team Player?

The most important activities of the church organist are those which involve the participation of others.

Hymns, chants, and liturgical responses should be considered top priority. These are the heart of the worship service and involve the entire congregation. Badly played accompaniments will upset a churchful of people. The wise organist plans congregational accompaniments with care and practices them with diligence.

Choir accompaniments rank next in importance. An inept accompaniment can make the entire choir, and its director, look and sound very bad.

Organ voluntaries are of third priority, but very meaningful in the total worship service. Play real music. Do not be content to provide pious "Muzak," "preludes-to-greet-friends-by," aural anaesthesia to ease any pain at the lifting of the offering. Play real music.

Personal Preferences vs. Job Priorities

Unfortunately, the organist sometimes sees an exactly reversed order of priorities. Many spend practically all of their practice time on organ solos, because they find these musically more interesting. Considerably less time may be spent on anthem accompaniments, and often little or none on the hymns and responses, which are read at sight in the service.

Such a lack of interest in the accompanist's role is perhaps a carry-over of conservatory-type training, which generally puts undue emphasis on the soloist's role while greatly undervaluing that of the accompanist or ensemble player. The musician who aspires to a career as a church organist, but dislikes to play accompaniments, is as innocent of reality as James Thurber's ingénue who longed to be a femme fatale, if she could do so "without getting mixed up with men."

Where the organist finds accompaniments dull work, it may be that he is playing them in a dull and tiresome manner. There is no valid excuse (except lack of interest) for an organist to play five or six successive hymn stanzas in an identical manner. Surely an understanding of the text being sung will suggest some variation.

Professional Cooperation and Consideration

Common-sense ground rules will help to smooth the operation of the director-accompanist leadership team.

Allow Time for Preparation. The organist, weeks in advance of performance, should receive listings of all anthems and hymns scheduled for the coming unit. In return, the director has every right to expect that accompaniments will be thoroughly prepared. Both director and accompanist ought to be ready to give maximum help to the choir at the very first reading of new music in rehearsal. Those who are "learning it along with the choir" simply are in no position to be really helpful.

If the director is considering an anthem with a very difficult accompaniment, he should discuss it with the organist before finalizing his schedule. There is nothing gained by humiliating or embarrassing the organist before the choir.

Work Out Problems Together. It is often desirable for the director and organist to study new music together. Both will benefit from mutual advance preparation, and in full rehearsal can concentrate their undivided attention on the problems encountered by the singers.

The accompanist must never publicly challenge the interpretations of the director, although in private the musical alternatives should be discussed freely. The leadership team must in public present a united front.

The registration of the organ for choral accompaniments should be most carefully worked out and tested. The organist should record the acceptable registration on his copy of each anthem (don't trust to memory), and no change from this should be made without the specific approval of the choir director.

Fixing Responsibility for Organ Maintenance

The pipe organ is a major financial investment for the congregation, often second only to the cost of the church building itself. The pipe organ should receive regular tuning and checkups. Far better to keep it in first-class condition than to await breakdowns which require repairs on an emergency basis.

Usually, both annoyance and expense can be minimized if organ servicing is contracted for on a regular basis, with an experienced individual or reputable firm. The director of music, the organist, and the music committee all have a direct interest in keeping the instrument in good operating order. Unfortunately, each may assume that organ maintenance is being handled by the others. A clear understanding of who is responsible for what is a good first step.

No matter who arranges the contract, the organist should keep written notes of all items that need attention. He should also try to be on hand when the technicians are working on the instrument.

EMPLOYING PROFESSIONAL SINGERS IN THE CHOIR

Define the Role of Professionals

Before hiring professional voices for the choir, the director should clarify in his own mind what he expects them to do for his church music program.

If professionals will be used primarily to sing solos, a distinctive and strong voice would be a logical first preference. However, such a voice might be difficult to blend into an ensemble.

If the main purpose is to strengthen the choral ensemble, one might prefer a less outstanding voice, coupled with superior musicianship.

Fortunately, many experienced professionals are able to sing effectively both in solo and ensemble. Others, usually with operatic or theatrical ambitions, have little interest or incentive to master the special art of ensemble singing; these can be troublesome.

A soloist should not be selected solely on the basis of voice and musicianship. Especially in church music, a pleasant personality and a cooperative attitude are fully as important as a fine voice. The abrasive personality can be as disruptive in a church choir as an abrasive voice.

Auditioning the Applicants

Auditioning professional singers, whether for a permanent church position or for a special program, requires tact and judgement. Young and inexperienced applicants may not be able to give you a fair impression of their true abilities in a brief try-out.

As far as possible, auditions should be held under performance conditions, not studio conditions. This will give a more accurate assessment of the singer's capabilities. Let the applicant first sing something he wishes you to hear. He should then sing something less familiar to him, which you wish to hear, even if it is a simple hymn tune.

During and after the audition, remain courteous, completely attentive, sympathetic, friendly, but non-committal. Do everything reasonable to put the singer at ease, but give no indication of your reaction until you have had a chance to hear all of the applicants.

After you do reach a decision, advise each applicant in writing, thanking each for his interest in trying out. Express no opinions, criticisms, or suggestions unless the applicant specifically requests it. Even then, great tact must be exercised; you are not his teacher, nor coach, nor a music critic. No one will profit from gratuitous advice which may be quite contrary to what the soloist is being taught by his instructor.

Opportunity May Be as Important as Salary

Money is important to church soloists, but it is seldom the sole motivation. Most soloists sing because they love to sing; in song they fulfill their personalities and express their emotions.

For many soloists, an interesting and challenging music program is fully as important as financial compensation. (This is equally true of accompanists.) The serious musician always wants to widen his musical horizon and gain experience in unfamiliar repertory. The soloist wants a chance to be heard under favorable musical circumstances; he wishes to be associated with a program that is both interesting and innovative.

The director should be prepared to show applicants the type of music the choir has been singing and outline his plans for the future growth of his program.

Being Considerate to Soloists

It will probably take some weeks for the director to determine accurately his soloists' abilities and limitations. Not all soloists have equal facility in reading or learning new music. Not all possess exceptional vocal range. The director must be sympathetic with the soloist's capabilities and at all times keep his demands within these limits.

Solos selected should always show the voice to best advantage. Do not ask the soloist to sight-read in rehearsal; allow ample time for preparation in private. Sudden surprises and last-minute changes have no place in a well-regulated church music program.

If your soloists are really good, they will, of course, have opportunities to sing elsewhere. Outside engagements may sometimes conflict with the soloist's obligation to you. Nonetheless, it is usually best to allow him to accept. Outside engagements are most important to a rising soloist's career. Further, his appearance may reflect favorably upon your own church's music program.

Professionals Should Supplement, Not Supplant

If the professionals sing all of the solos, there is no opportunity in the choir for the talented volunteer singer who has solo ambitions. Yet, some professionals may resent sitting by while those with less training and experience sing solos.

A well-organized church music program should foster the artistic growth and development of all participants. If professionals are also the section leaders, they should assist and encourage the volunteer choir members in every way, including help in preparing an occasional incidental solo. It must be remembered that church members sponsor, support, and finance the music program. The talented church members who sing in the choir should be able to participate to the fullest extent of their abilities.

It is best if the director makes it clear at the very start that professionals have been engaged to supplement the volunteer singers, not to supplant them.

CHOIR ORGANIZATION AND CHOIR OFFICERS

Formal Organization or "Family Style"

In a choir of fewer than 30 members, not a great deal of formal organization is required; such groups can operate effectively "family style," with a minimum of official bureaucracy. With a flexible and non-formal setup, the most interested and capable individuals assume appropriate functions as volunteers or are drafted into service by the director. Larger choirs, however, will almost certainly do better with a more formal organizational structure: an official constitution and bylaws, specific requirements for membership, and an annual election of choir officers.[1]

The director's chief concern with any type of organizational structure is that it works well enough to free him from recurrent non-musical chores. Thus all of his time can be devoted to his musical responsibilities. In making music, the process is more significant than the structure.

Organizational Form Should Follow Function

A church choir is not a business organization; a president, vice-president, secretary, treasurer, etc. may or may not be relevant to the real functions of the choir. Perhaps officers' titles should conform closely to their actual services. In nearly all church choirs, the indispensable people are librarians, section leaders, and robe mothers.

Librarians should have complete responsibility for the choir's music:

- They assign music folios to the choir members.
- They distribute and retrieve music copies.
- They mark changes in the copies as requested by the director.
- They repair damaged octavos or order replacements.
- They maintain the stacks or files where music is stored.

Section leaders correspond to the principals in orchestral sections:

- They provide a correct musical model for others.
- They advise the director of special needs or problems in their section.
- They may call and conduct special sectional rehearsals.
- They help recruit new singers.
- They help new members to settle in.
- The best singer in the section is not necessarily the ideal section leader in a church choir. The most effective leader is likely to be an experienced member, with superior musicianship and a personality that naturally commands respect. Where

---

[1]Several church denominational headquarters have model constitutions for church choirs.

professional singers are hired, they may be ex officio section leaders.

Robe mothers or wardrobe chairmen look after the choir's vestments:

- They assign robes to choir members.
- They make small repairs to the robes.
- They arrange for regular cleaning of the vestments.
- In children's choirs, they may assist the director in keeping order.
- In large choirs, several robe mothers may be needed.

One should be on hand at every choir appearance.

MOBILIZING THE INSTRUMENTAL RESOURCES

Ad Hoc Groups Are Practical Everywhere

In nearly every congregation there is a reservoir of untapped instrumental talent whose participation could add much to the church music program. This talent too often is unused, simply because the administrator of the music program does not know it is there or does not take the trouble to incorporate these musicians into his program.

The first step towards an effective instrumental program is an inventory of instrumental resources. By inquiry, invitation, or congregational questionnaire, the director should somehow learn who plays what instrument, and how well.

The simplest program is the use of instruments on an ad hoc basis. The director keeps an up-to-date file of available players. He then schedules choral-instrumental numbers or instrumental solos and ensembles, utilizing the available talent. Each player is advised in advance when he is scheduled to rehearse and perform.

Possible Permanent Ensembles

Brass choirs were highly developed in European churches as early as the 16th century. Much of the published literature for brass choirs is beyond the ability of students or average players. But it is not difficult to make transcriptions tailored exactly to the players and instruments available, and to the occasion of use.

Brass choirs alone are effective, but are even more so when teamed with organ and percussion. Antiphonal numbers for chorus and brass choirs also offer exceptionally interesting musical possibilities.

String ensembles and small orchestras were, during the 18th century, a feature of nearly every cathedral, large church, or chapel of nobility in Europe. The Kapellmeister was expected to be skilled with both choral and instrumental ensembles. Nearly all of the choral music of composers such as Buxtehude, Bach, Vivaldi, Handel, Haydn, and Mozart was conceived for performance with voices and orchestra, not for chorus alone, nor chorus with organ. Their music is greatly enhanced when presented with the original scoring for small orchestra.

If much 18th century music is to be performed, it might be possible to organize a small but dependable ensemble. As few as six players can be very effective: four violins, one viola, one cello. A string ensemble of nine can balance nicely a chorus of up to 40 voices: five violins, two violas, one cello, one contrabass. Winds and tympani, where called for in the score, should be used if available, but are seldom absolutely essential.

In much 18th century music, instrumental parts are widely interchangeable between strings and winds: violin parts can be played on flutes, recorders, or oboes; parts for cellos can be played by bassoons or bass recorders.

Pop—folk—gospel combos represent a strong trend in contemporary church music. There is a rising flood of hymns and liturgies in the pop-music idiom. Much of this is ersatz folk-style and painfully amateurish. (This should not be wondered at when the "composers" can't read a note of music!) Whatever his opinions concerning the quality of the music, the director cannot afford to ignore any trend or development in worship music. He should be as well-informed about the music of his own time as he is concerning the music of any other period.

Appropriate accompaniment for pop-folk music can be a problem. The pipe organ is simply too sedate to be suitable. Acoustic guitars, while perhaps suitable, are too weak in volume of sound for use in a large church. The most practical instruments might be piano, amplified guitar, electric bass, and percussion. A choir backed by such a combo can make some interesting and exciting music.

Jazz bands are the best accompaniment when Dixieland or jazz idioms are used in church. The basis of jazz sound is a lively rhythm, set by piano and drum-set, possibly aided by banjo. To these can be added almost any available wind instruments.

A handbell choir has found a place among the musical ensembles in some churches. Handbells are purchased in matched sets; they are a substantial financial investment. Tunes are played by groups of ringers who clang the properly pitched bells in sequence. The musical potential of handbells is somewhat limited, but no great musical skill is necessary, either. Handbells are often played by the older children in a multiple-choir program. There is a growing literature for handbells alone, or in combination with voices and organ.

Orff-type ensembles of recorders, xylophones, marimbas, chimes, and glockenspiels, accompanied by rhythm instruments such as drums, cymbals, triangles, wood-blocks, and bells, have great possibilities in church music. Such ensembles are something of a novelty in American churches, but are to be found in public schools all over the world.

The Carl Orff concept of music instruction stresses the development of creativity and musical imagination in the performers, usually children. However, there is absolutely no reason why adults should be excluded from experimenting and performing on these delightful instruments.[2]

Special Orff-type instruments can be purchased from school-music supply houses. However, standard marimbas, vibraharps, and xylophones certainly can be used.

MUSIC WHEN THE CHOIR IS OFF-DUTY

Music Is Meaningful at Minor Services, Too

The comprehensive church music program ought to provide music for the services at which the full choir is not expected to appear. These may be prayer meetings, midweeks, or summer services. Music for these smaller services can best be provided by small ensembles of singers or instrumentalists.

The director should include in the church music library a special section of music which is appropriate for these smaller groups.

Encouraging and Developing Musical Leadership

Within the church choir, there are usually some members who

---

[2]*Settings of Chorales for Treble Voices,* edited by Mandus Egge, published by Augsburg Publishing House, 1969, code 11-9382, contains ten examples of classic chorales enlivened by Orff-style accompaniments. A study of these will surely suggest other possibilities for the Orff instrumental ensemble.

have a special interest in small ensemble singing. Also, in the congregation, there may be musical people who cannot be active as full-time choir members, but who would enjoy ensemble singing on occasion.

The director himself may assume the leadership of these ensembles. But in many cases these afford a fine opportunity for members of the choir to develop their own leadership abilities. Under the supervision of the director, a capable chorister should be encouraged to organize an ensemble for a specific occasion at church, select the music, conduct the rehearsals, and direct the ensemble in performance.

Those who participate in a small ensemble usually (as a bonus) show an increased interest in the total church music program as well. Perhaps this is because they have found a special niche in it for themselves.

COMMUNICATING IDEAS AND INFORMATION

Two-Way Communication Is Vital

An effective communication system should be as carefully organized as any phase of the director's musical activities.

The communication system should encourage and facilitate the flow of information and ideas in both directions: to the director and from the director. The music department can scarcely function at all unless the administrator's plans and programs are clearly understood by all participants. But it is equally important that the director know what the participants are thinking. He must be open and responsive to the opinions and ideas of others who have an interest in the church's music.

From the director's viewpoint, the communication problem may be seen as a series of concentric circles.

a. *The inmost circle* includes only those who manage or direct the musical program: conductors and accompanists. Interchange in this circle should be frequent, free, and informal.

b. *The second circle* includes all of the participants in the music program: choristers, soloists, instrumentalists, librarians, choir mothers.

c. *The third circle* includes those who have a direct interest in the program, but are not performers: the pastor, music committee, church office secretary, building custodian, and others who are directly or indirectly involved with music activities.

d. *The outer circle* in the communication system includes the potential audience: the congregation, and sometimes the community at large.

Specific lines of communication should be set up to reach the groups within each of these circles.

Using Both Eye-Gate and Ear-Gate

Some business organizations enforce an excellent rule for all employees: *Accept no verbal instructions.* This is a fundamental concept in communications, and one which prevents a great many misunderstandings which could result in incorrect action.

The object in communicating is to achieve a clear and mutual understanding. One should never assume that his every pronouncement is so lucid that it is immediately grasped by every listener. But one can be reasonably certain of understanding if he sends the message through both the eye-gate and the ear-gate. Use the following in communicating:

- Written memos.
- Oral repetition (for reinforcement).
- Brief discussion (for clarification).

  If you wish to announce an important extra rehearsal:
- Write the message on the chalkboard (eye-gate).
- Read the message aloud during the rehearsal break (ear-gate).
- Ask for questions, comments, or discussion.

Similarly, in communicating with the congregation, a written message in the church bulletin or a poster in the foyer should be reinforced by an oral announcement from the lectern.

BASIC COMMUNICATION TOOLS

The Hymn Schedule

Hymns, psalms, and liturgical responses are sometimes selected by the pastor, sometimes by the director of music, but most successfully in conference by both. If at all possible, hymns should be programmed, not from Sunday to Sunday, but in units of about 14 to 18 weeks.

However the hymns are selected, the director of music should provide everyone who is interested with a printed copy of the *hymn schedule.* This shows which hymns, psalms, and service music will be used each Sunday in the next unit. (See Illustration 2-1, next page.)

Hymns for Lent and Easter Season

Date and Occasion	Hymnal Number	Title
March 2	354	Beneath the cross of Jesus
1st in Lent	219	In the hour of trial
	92	Psalm 130
March 9	61	When in the hour of utmost
2nd in Lent		need
	55	My song is love unknown
	78	Psalm 25

Illustration 2-1

The hymn schedule is a key to improved hymn-singing.

Organists can prepare interesting hymn preludes or intonations. They can prepare accompaniments that are appropriate to each stanza of each hymn.

The director can schedule choral music which is compatible with the hymn selections. He can prepare the choir in rehearsal to give good leadership to the congregation. He can plan variations in hymn-singing: descants, faux-bourdon, antiphonal stanzas, unusual instrumental accompaniments.

The pastor may wish to cite stanzas of these hymns in his sermons, or to reflect the thought of the hymns in his pastoral prayer.

Church school leaders can include the study and performance of these hymns in the teaching curriculum.

The Choral Music Schedule

A second vital communications tool is the *Choral Music Schedule.* Choral music should be programmed in advance for logical portions of the church year, perhaps 14 to 18 weeks in a unit. A list of the music selected for performance should be printed and distributed to all participants in the music program, and to all who are interested in it (the first three circles in the communications system). (See Illustration 2-2.)

```
┌─────────────────────────────────────────────────────────┐
│                                                         │
│        Choral Music for Advent, Christmas, Epiphany     │
│                                                         │
```

Date and Occasion	Composer	Title
Nov. 30 1st in Advent	Brahms/Klein G. Holst	The angel's greeting Let all mortal flesh
Dec. 7 2nd in Advent	P. Christiansen Franck/Buszin	My Song in the night Oh Jesus grant me hope

Illustration 2-2

Rehearsal accompanists can prepare in advance, and can assist the choir greatly from the very first reading in rehearsal.

Organists can prepare musicianly accompaniments.

The director can assign all solos and arrange for any special instrumental accompaniments. He can use the schedule as a weekly rehearsal guide.

The choristers are able to do private rehearsal, and thus conserve group-rehearsal time. Some will arrange personal affairs so they will not miss the performance of a favorite piece.

The pastor can effectively incorporate in his sermon the great spiritual ideas which have been sung by the choir. This helps to unify the service, and increases the impact of both the anthem and the sermon.

The church office secretary has the information she needs each week to make up her service bulletin. She will also appreciate it if the organist will provide her with a similar unit plan for preludes and postludes.

The Choir Newsletter

A most effective inter-departmental communications tool is the *Choir Newsletter.* This can be published weekly, monthly, or seasonally (Advent, Epiphany, Lent, etc.).

It should be understood by all that the announcements and information in the newsletter are "official" and that no follow-up individual notes or reminders are to be expected.

The newsletter can be printed on the office duplicator and mailed by the church secretarial staff.

Emphasize in the letter the good news, the upbeat, the positive and encouraging. Singers will not look forward to receiving a letter filled with defeatism, pessimism, and complaints. News items should be brief, pertinent to the choir's purpose, and adapted to rapid reading and comprehension. Try to include:

- *Names* (everyone likes to see his in print).
- *News* about choir members: activities, events.
- *Coming events:* who, what, where, when, why.
- *Program notes* about music in rehearsal.
- *Suggestions* about singing or music in general.
- *Community music news:* concerts, recitals.
- *Comment* on past performance of the choir.
- *Recognition* of soloists, accompanists, instrumentalists.
- *Fan mail* for the choir, if you get any.
- *Announcements* by librarians, robe mothers.
- *Anecdotes* and jokes about music or church affairs.
- *Notes* from the pastor or church officials.
- *Biographical notes* about composers, authors.

The Annual Report

The director of music may be required to submit to the administration a summary of the music departmental activities. An adequate and accurate records-keeping system is an invaluable source of such information.

Even if the church administration does not insist on such a summary, it is most helpful if the director compiles one for his own use. A study of the membership and attendance statistics can point up the problems which need his attention.

A Choir Yearbook or Anniversary Book

As photocopy equipment becomes more readily available in churches, the publication of an interesting, illustrated yearbook becomes increasingly practical.

The yearbook may contain:

- Annualized attendance and membership statistics.
- Choir roster, with years of service indicated.
- Pictures and data on music department personnel, officers, librarians, section leaders, etc.
- Activity reports from each musical organization.
- Reviews of special musical events.
- Pictures of musical activities, informal and formal.

As an alternative to annual books, anniversary books have much to recommend them. These can be published in conjunction with a significant event in the life of the local congregation:

- Dedication of a new organ.
- Dedications of a new building.
- 25th, 50th, or 100th anniversary of the congregation.
- An important anniversary of the pastor.

Reaching the Congregation Through the Church Bulletin

Music department news should be consistently included in the church bulletin and in the church's press releases to local news media.

a. Make sure that the name and title of each choir director and accompanist is included in the directory of church personnel.

b. Rehearsal times for each choir should be listed regularly in the calendar of church activities.

c. All music performed in the service should be correctly identified in the service bulletin.

d. Wherever possible, have anthem texts printed in the bulletin; eye-gate and ear-gate communication.

e. Write a regular "Music Corner" for the bulletin. Include brief program notes about the music to be performed. These will increase the congregation's appreciation of the music.

Personalized Memo Pads

The director can create a favorable and business-like impression by the use of personally imprinted memo pads. These can be made up by the local print-shop, and should show

Your Name	Title
Home Address	Name of Church
Home Phone	Address of Church
	Church Phone

These can be used for all personal notes relating to the church music program: to fellow musicians or pastor, orders to music dealers, confirmation to hired musicians, requests to publishers for materials on approval or catalogs, "thank you" notes, "get well" wishes, congratulations and condolences, invitations to new members.

The value of individual, personal attention to one's associates cannot be overestimated. We all respond best to those who show a sincere interest in us as people.

3 Building and Maintaining an Adequate Choir

CREATING YOUR OWN CHORAL INSTRUMENT

Choirs Are Made by Conductors

The conductor of a church choir must design, build, and maintain his own musical instrument. Mechanical musical instruments, such as pianos, organs, or harpsichords, can be bought. But the choir is an instrument composed of human personalities which must be won. While a mechanical instrument will respond well to any player who handles the keys proficiently, the choir is so sensitive and so ephemeral an instrument that a change in the facial expression of the conductor will make an immediate change in the sound of the choir—for better or worse.

The congregation cannot deliver to the director a finished, ready-made choir. At best, it can offer potential. The director must be able to design and build a choir for himself or else he will never be able to conduct one.

The principal component of the church choir is the average person with an ordinary voice. A choral conductor who knows his business can build a good choir in a poor congregation or a rich one, in the inner city, or suburb, or small town.

The Church Choir Is Always "Under Construction"

Maintaining a church choir is literally a never ending task. Attrition of membership is continual, and must be matched by constant recruiting to forestall disintegration.

The turnover of singers in the choir usually reflects the mobility and change in the congregation. Singers grow up, go off to school, marry, move away, take time out to have babies, change jobs, work on different shifts, travel, and grow too old to sing. Eventually, you lose them all.

An annual membership loss of 20 to 30% is typical in many metropolitan areas. With a choir of 25 voices, this may mean that five or seven new singers must be recruited each year, just to hold the membership level. If the choir is to show some slight growth, eight or ten new members would have to be found each year.

Recruiting Is Everyone's Responsibility

The recruiting of singers is so essential to the success of the church choir that there is never a question about whether or not to do it. The only question is how best to recruit. Some directors have found this to be the most vexing and difficult problem they face.

It should not be necessary for the director to shoulder this entire burden. If the choir is important to the whole church, the entire congregation should be willing to work to maintain choir membership. Successful recruiting requires the cooperation of all: clergy, music committee, choir members, music staff, and the entire congregation. The director should take the lead in organizing and supervising the recruiting effort. But he should not be expected to do all of the work alone; it is, in fact, impossible for him to do so.

DESIGNING A CHOIR TO FIT YOUR CHURCH

Choirs, Like Organs, Should Be Custom-Designed

Before the director starts to construct his choir he should create a rational design, envisioning the type of choir he wishes to have. A choir, like an organ, should be individually designed for the church in which it will serve. Choir-builders and organ-builders basically must consider similar factors and limitations: congregational resources, probable musical repertory, and the architecture and acoustics of the church auditorium.

Expect 5% of the Congregation to Be in Choir

The size of the congregation determines the size of the choir. A reasonable expectation is that approximately 5% of the active adult membership will participate in the choir. A church of 500 members should afford a choir of 25 to 30 voices. With children and youth, participation in choir is usually much higher, attracting 10 to 25% of the eligible children, and often much more.

Fitting the Choir to the Repertory

The type of music to be sung will greatly influence the design of the choir. In general, the total size of a choir is of less significance than the choral balance. Where the repertory is primarily polyphonic, the voice sections must be meticulously matched in volume and texture of sound, regardless of the total size of the ensemble; a domineering soprano section is a built-in disaster. In classic polyphony, a small, precisely balanced choir has every advantage, as most of this music was written expressly for such groups.

On the other hand, if most of the repertory will be homophonic gospel songs and choruses, a very different choral design might be appropriate. In such music, a "big" sound and enthusiastic participation are more to be sought than delicacy and musical finesse. The gospel-type choir should be as large as possible, with an especially strong soprano section to give prominence to the melodic line.

Where the choral repertory is varied, the director should design a versatile and adaptable choir. The key is *adaptability,* so that, within reason, singers should expect to be placed where they are most needed in each composition: second soprano or first alto; second tenor or baritone.

In the versatile SATB choir, not less than 20% nor more than 30% of the total membership should be in any one voice section. If voices total 25, there should be at least five in the weakest section, and not more than eight in the strongest.

The Effect of Architecture and Acoustics on Choir Design

The size of the choir should be matched to the size of the sanctuary. A delicately balanced polyphonic choir of six to ten voices is most effective in an intimate chapel. A choir of 50 sounds best in a large auditorium or cathedral-type of sanctuary.

Choirs sound best when they sing directly to the congregation. An enormous amount of sound is lost if they face away from the congregation. Thus, a divided choir loft, where the singers face each other instead of facing the congregation, is so acoustically inefficient that it requires many more singers than a more rational arrangement.[1]

---

[1]This matter is discussed at greater length in Chapter 4, p. 86.

Good Choirs Come in All Sizes

What is the optimum size for a church choir? In the 16th century, the so-called "Golden Age of Choral Song," the choir of the Sistine Chapel was perhaps the finest in Europe. It numbered about 20 singers. In the 18th century, even very large churches and cathedrals had very small choirs, with two or three voices on each part. J.S. Bach's regular choir at Weimar consisted of six boys and six men. In 1729, for the first performance of his *St. Matthew Passion,* Bach's choir numbered 16, with an orchestra of 18. At the first performance of *The Messiah* in 1752, Handel used the choirs of the two leading churches in Dublin, St. Patrick's and Christchurch. The total combined membership of these two choirs was six boys and 14 men. Both boys and men in such choirs were well-trained professionals. But it is obvious that these ensembles produced no massive, high-decibel sound.

Perhaps the modern-day listener is conditioned to a more rich and full choral sound. Certainly the most successful choirs of our day are relatively large by the standards of past centuries. A clue to the optimum size for a present-day choir may be found in a comparison of professional touring choirs. These must produce a sonority acceptable in a hall seating 1,000 listeners or more. Yet, because of financial limitations, professional choirs carry no excess voices.

Robert Shaw built his reputation with a chorale of 32 voices: 20 men and 12 women. Fred Waring, in the late 1940's and early 1950's, toured with an excellent choir of 22: 17 men and 5 women. Roger Wagner and Norman Luboff have appeared on the concert circuit with choirs of 24 to 28 voices.

It would appear that optimum choral efficiency is reached with something like 25 to 30 voices. This choir size is well within the reach of the congregation of 500 members.

Beautiful music is of course possible with much smaller ensembles, but two points must be borne in mind:

- The smaller the choir, the more perfect must be each voice.
- Repertory must be carefully matched to the lesser sonority of the smaller group.

With volunteer singers of average ability, the addition of each single voice improves the sound of the section until an optimum is reached. Five voices sound much better than three; ten sound much better than five. However, 20 voices in a section will sound bigger, but not necessarily better than ten, demonstrating the law of diminishing returns. Optimum efficiency seems to be reached with about eight to ten sopranos, seven to eight altos, five to six tenors, and seven to eight basses.

Establishing Specific Membership Goals

In planning a recruiting program, the director should set specific membership goals for each voice section; growth should be controlled and matched to the overall needs of the choir. If there are already eight sopranos, three altos, two tenors, and two basses, the addition of four more sopranos will likely make the choir worse instead of better. Recruit, especially, the voices that are most urgently needed.

REVIEWING PREVIOUS RECRUITING METHODS

Procedures and Results of Previous Campaigns

Before undertaking a recruiting campaign, the director should review procedures and results of previous efforts.

What changes have occurred since the last recruiting effort?

	yes	no
A new pastor?	——	——
A new music committee?	——	——
Evident change in the congregation?	——	——

Who helped in the previous effort?

Clergy?	——	——
Music committee?	——	——
Choir members?	——	——
Other music staff members?	——	——

To what groups have recruiting messages been addressed?

Congregation at large?	——	——
To those with known musical interests?	——	——

To new members of the congregation? ___ ___

To youth? ___ ___

To men? ___ ___

To women? ___ ___

To families? ___ ___

Which motivations were emphasized?

Self-interest, personal satisfaction? ___ ___

Unselfish service to the church? ___ ___

Opportunity for musical experience? ___ ___

Enjoyable social activities? ___ ___

Other? ___ ___

What communication was used?

Announcements in church? ___ ___

Phone calls? ___ ___

Personal visits? ___ ___

Notices in church bulletin? ___ ___

Direct mail? ___ ___

Posters and bulletin boards? ___ ___

Other? ___ ___

What were the tangible results?

How many new singers joined the choir? _____

How many seemed responsive, but did
not join immediately? _____

Solicit Suggestions and Participation

As the director gathers data on past campaigns, he should also seek suggestions for improving the recruiting effort. Comment and new ideas should be sought from the clergy, music committee, music staff members, and choir singers. In contacting these people, the director should emphasize that:

- A strong choir benefits the total church program.
- The cooperation of all is necessary for a successful recruiting effort.
- The active assistance of all is expected.

PROGRAMMED RECRUITING

Recruit Regularly; Don't Wait for Trouble

Sooner or later, every present member of your choir will depart, and a replacement will be needed. It is much easier to keep the choir at full strength by adding a few new voices regularly than it is to await a serious shortage, and then try in desperation to induct a large number of new singers.

With a church choir, as with an automobile, systematic maintenance can avert embarrassing breakdowns and costly overhaul. The systematic recruitment of new choir members should be programmed into the director's yearly cycle of normal activities.

A Practical Plan: Three Enrollments Each Year

Three brief but intense recruiting drives each year should be sufficient to maintain choir membership. These drives can be timed to anticipate the major festivals of the church year.

First enrollment, early September. Many church choirs resume a full schedule of activities after Labor Day. Singers joining at this time can anticipate the major religious observances ahead: Thanksgiving, Reformation, All Saints', Advent, and Christmas.

Second enrollment, after Christmas. With the Christmas season, interest in religious music reaches a high point. At this time, many churches also receive new members, who should be specifically invited to participate in the musical activities. Ahead are the great services and special programs for Lent, Holy Week, and Easter.

Third enrollment, after Easter. Nearly all churches receive new members at this season. New members for the choir should be most welcome at this time. Ahead lie the festivals of Pentecost and Trinity, with special musical possibilities. Also ahead are the summer vacation months, when help will be most appreciated in offsetting an increasing rate of absenteeism.

New choir members are usually welcome at any time. But recruiting efforts should be confined to specific enrollment periods.

Appeal to Basic Motivations for Choir Membership

The recruiting campaign should set forth in a clear and forceful manner, the benefits, advantages, and opportunities of choir membership. These are musical, spiritual, and social.

Musical Motivations

For many adults, church choir is the only available outlet for employing musical abilities.
Opportunity for further musical training and growth.
Performing choral masterworks; appreciating these as doers, not as hearers only.

Spiritual Motivations

Christian commitment expressed in personal service.
Assisting in an important church function.
Opportunity for intensive study of great Scriptural texts; spiritual insights interpreted through music.
Talents used increase; talents buried are lost.
(Matthew 24:14-30).

Social Motivations

Enjoy group activity, fellowship.
Meet new people.
Enjoy performing in public.
Opportunity for self-expression, recognition.
Family activity: father, mother, and youth can all participate on an equal basis.

A THREE-PHASE RECRUITING EFFORT

First-Phase Recruiting: Publicity

The recruiting campaign should be completed within a two- or three-week period; prolonged efforts usually result in diminishing returns.

Publicity is the first phase of a recruiting campaign. Its purpose is to make every church member aware of the needs of the musical organizations, and of the advantages and benefits offered to those who participate in these activities. These messages can reach church members in numerous ways.

Announcements can be made by the pastor, the choir director, or by choir members at successive worship services. Supplementary notices can be read at meetings of church organizations: Bible classes, circles, clubs, and youth organizations. At these less formal events, questions or comments can be invited.

Notices in the church bulletin should supplement oral announcements. These should be very brief, giving the time and place of the next rehearsal. Each notice should include an invitation to specific action: Attend the next rehearsal or call for additional information.

Posters should be placed in the foyer or narthex. Choir members with artistic ability can make up attractive placards, urging specific action: Attend the rehearsal or call for additional information.

Second-Phase Recruiting: Special Materials

Publicity alone will seldom bring a flood of recruits for the choir; it merely lays the groundwork. To be effective, there must be follow-up to reach the individuals who might be interested. Special materials make this quite simple.

Contact Cards. Some prospects for choir might wish additional information before making a commitment to membership. When announcements are made at church, distribute "Contact Cards" with which interested prospects may request additional information about the music program. Contact cards can be printed on the church office duplicator. (See Illustration 3-1.)

```
Please give me additional information about

Adult choir _____ Children's choir _____

Youth choir _____ Instrumental groups _____

Name . . . . . . . . . . . . . . Phone . . . . .

Address . . . . . . . . . . . . . . . . . . . . . .
```

Illustration 3-1

Direct Mail. A form letter from the pastor and the director of music can be sent to each church family. This should briefly describe the music program, with the opportunities offered for each age group, and encourage participation. Always suggest a positive response: Attend the next rehearsal or mail the enclosed Contact Card for additional information.

Music Department Brochure. A pamphlet describing or picturing the activities of the church music organizations can be developed. The pamphlet should:

- Describe each organization, listing qualifications for membership.
- Outline the specific activities planned for the coming season.
- List the time and place for rehearsals and the church services at which the organization appears.

Brochures can be distributed at church services, in conjunction with recruiting announcements. They may also be mailed to the homes of parishioners.

Third-Phase Recruiting: The Music Survey

At times, the director may be faced with the problem of establishing an entirely new music program, or rebuilding a badly deteriorated one. Before undertaking this, he should make a careful assessment of the true musical potential of the congregation. A "Church Music Survey" will accomplish this.

To conduct a survey, the director will need the help of those who have a personal knowledge of the church membership: the clergy, parish worker, church secretary, members of the music committee. Together, these people should study the complete church membership roll, identifying each parishioner or parish family that has evidenced a musical interest of any kind. Look for families where someone—

- Has previously sung in choir.
- Takes music lessons.
- Plays a musical instrument of any kind.
- Sings in a school or community chorus.
- Sings in a "barbershop" group.
- Enjoys singing hymns in church.

A "Church Music Survey Form" should be prepared for each such person or family. The survey form can be printed on the church office duplicator. The name, address, and phone number of each musical family should be filled in at the church office. (See Illustration 3-2.)

Church Music Survey Report

Name (supplied at church office)   Phone (supplied)
Address (supplied)   Date of call _____

1. Are any adults interested in singing in choir?

        What is now preventing them from doing so?

2. Are any children interested in singing in choir?

        What is now preventing them from doing so?

3. Does any member of the family play an instrument?

        Player's name _____

        Instrument _____
        Any interest in playing in church ensemble?

Illustration 3-2

The survey will be more productive if preceded by a vigorous campaign of publicity. This will alert the congregation to the survey and help insure a positive response.

Choir members can be enlisted as survey reporters. Each reporter should have three to five families to contact. Calls should be completed within one week and all survey forms returned immediately to the director. Calls may be made in person or by telephone.

Best results are obtained if the director personally follows up each interested prospect immediately. If an interested prospect cannot immediately join the choir, retain his survey report for future follow-up.

Clarifying the Commitment: Choir Registration Cards

Enroll singers in the choir with "Choir Registration Cards," especially designed for this purpose. The registration card serves three purposes:

- Provides current personnel information.
- Confirms to the singer the dates of choir appearances.
- Solicits information desired by the director.

Registration cards should be newly revised at the start of each new music unit. A standard 4 X 6-inch index card works well and can be imprinted on the office duplicator. (See Illustration 3-3.)

Choir Registration Card

Name _____ Phone _____

Address _____

Voice Part _____ Highest note _____ Lowest _____

Please cross off services listed below at which you will *not* be able to sing. Advise promptly if plans change.

January	*February*	*March*
3	7	7
10	14	14
17	21	21
24	24 (Ash Wed.)	28
31	28	

April 4   Palm Sunday _____ 8:00 p.m.   cantata _____
April 11   Easter   Sunrise Service _____ Regular Service _____

Interested in solo work?
Interested in small ensemble singing?
Comments or suggestions:

Illustration 3-3

    The registration card is an informal contract between the singer and the choir. It shows him when he is expected to sing and gives him a chance to advise the director in advance when he cannot. Surprisingly, choir members seem to know pretty well in advance when business trips, vacations, school, or family affairs will necessitate their absence from choir. It is very important that the director be aware of (for example) an impending exodus of singers over the Easter holidays. It could make a great deal of difference in the kind of music he would schedule for that festive occasion.

PLACING VOICES IN THE CHOIR

Help Each to Fulfill His Aspirations

Church choir members comprise a very diverse group, differing widely in age and musical ability. It is the task of the church choirmaster to help this heterogeneous group perform music together, beautifully and effectively. To do this, he will need a practical knowledge of choral technique and superior teaching skills. But even more than technical skills, the director of the church choir needs to understand and love his people as much as he understands and loves his music. He must be sensitive to the needs, ambitions, and emotional drives of each individual singer. Insofar as he is capable, the director should help each person in his choir to develop his talent and fulfill his musical aspirations.

In the very finest sense, the church choir director is to be, not the master, but truly the servant of all.

Excellent Choirs Created from Average Voices

Most church choir singers have average, ordinary voices. A few are better, a few are worse than average. But this does not mean that the choir is foredoomed to mediocrity; far from it. Choral singing is synergetic: the result is much greater than the mere sum of individual effort. In solo performance, the ordinary voice may be pleasant, but not particularly exciting. But 30 ordinary voices, with proper discipline, can become a musical instrument of surpassing beauty with enormous potential for musical expression.

If there is anything exceptional about the average choir singer, it is his attitude, not his voice. Given an ordinary voice, the really important qualifications of a chorister are:

- A desire to sing.
- A desire to serve.
- A willingness to learn.
- A cheerful, cooperative spirit.
- Subordination of self to group effort.

The effectiveness of the choir will be determined by the singers' attitudes rather than by their vocal aptitudes.

To Test, or not to Test?

Are vocal try-outs or placement tests essential in a church choir? Certainly the directors of college or professional choirs would consider them so, as their singers are almost always selected through competitive auditions.

It must be remembered, however, that these directors are attempting to select the very best from a number of candidates. Their tests have been devised to help them do this efficiently and quickly. The director of the church choir, however, seldom finds himself in the position of selecting his singers from a large surplus of applicants. In many instances, a nervous, ill-at-ease amateur simply cannot give the director a fair impression of his ability in an audition. If held at all, such auditions should be considered tentative at best, and certainly no substitute for continual close observation of each singer (and especially new singers) in actual rehearsal and performance.

Each chorister is an absolutely unique personality, with his individual strengths and weaknesses. Abilities and attitudes undergo continual change. It is up to the director to observe everything and guide each singer into his correct place in the church choir.

Assign Voices Where Each Will Do the Most Good

To preserve the choral balance, the director must at times exercise arbitrary judgement in the placing of voices in the choir. Many women could sing a second soprano part as easily as a first alto part. The singer's preference merits reasonable consideration, but should not take precedence over the needs of the team. Each singer should understand that she will be assigned, and perhaps later re-assigned wherever she will be of greatest value to the choir.

As a matter of convenience, composers have traditionally classified voices as soprano, alto, tenor, and bass. When one considers the whole range of human voices, these classifications are at best inadequate and arbitrary. Nature bestows an infinite variety of voices, not just four, differing in both range and quality of sound. Some, of course, are true soprano, true alto, true tenor, and true bass.

Perhaps the majority of ladies' voices could be described as mezzo; relatively few are "soprano" enough to pronounce clearly and easily on high G or A. Even more rare are true altos. Paul Christiansen once remarked that he could recall only two or three real altos in all of his years of choral conducting. One famous professional director, only half-joking, observed that most of his "altos" seemed to be the mezzos who smoked too much.

Correspondingly, most male voices are also "mezzo," in the

middle. True basses are surely as rare as true tenors. Gerhardt Schroth summed it up: "In most choirs, the basses are all baritones. The tenors are the baritones with guts!"

All singers in a volunteer choir should understand the importance of flexibility and adaptability. The baritone who can and will sing second tenor is a most valuable choir member. Fred Waring put it well from the viewpoint of the professional director when he said: "We expect good voices and good musicianship in applicants. What we look for, what we hire and pay for, is flexibility."

Helping New Singers to "Settle In"

Two or three new choir members can be accommodated into the choir at one time without any special problem. The director may simply introduce the new singers to the section leader, librarian, and robe chairman. These, in turn, see that the newcomer becomes acquainted with the other singers in the section, and is assigned a music folder and robe. At rehearsal, it is most helpful if newcomers sit between experienced veterans who can help them with choir procedures that might otherwise prove perplexing.

Five or six new members at one time, however, may be enough to upset or impede a rehearsal because of their inexperience. To avoid this possibility, the director may wish to organize an hour or two of basic instruction or orientation for a group of newcomers. Here the director can teach or review the basics of choral singing and explain procedures used in the choir.

Protecting the Character of the Individual Voice

Each voice is a unique voice. To the greatest possible extent, the integrity and character of the individual voice in the chorus should be protected, not "corrected" to conform to the director's pre-conceived notions of tone. While the director must certainly work for a reasonable assimilation of each new voice in the section, there is absolutely no need for total conformity. Anticipate that each new voice will make some change in the sound of the section, some change in the tonal palette, hopefully for the better. After all, there is no "one and only correct choral sound," any more than there is only one "correct" sound for a solo voice or only one "correct" organ stop.

Sectional Seating Affects Sectional Tone

The physical fact of who sits next to whom can make a very great difference in the sound of a voice section.

If seven sopranos are seated in the order of A, B, C, D, E, F, G, they will sound quite different as a section if re-seated A, G, C, F, E, B, D, and will change sound again if arranged B, G, A, F, C, D, E.

Each singer is affected by her neighbors, and will alter her singing in some way because of their presence. Certainly, there are psychological factors at work here. But there may also be physical factors, akin to sympathetic vibration, set in play by the juxtaposition of certain voices. Singers themselves are keenly aware that they sing better, or enjoy it more, if seated next to a certain partner. Ladies with strong voices and assertive personalities will often avoid sitting near each other in rehearsal. It should be understood that the director will assign seating to create the best sectional sound.

In general, mixing voice-types seems to work well. Seat the light, straight voice next to the strong, vibrant voice; the novice next to the veteran; the young singer next to an older one. Keep the dominant voices towards the rear of the section; certainly not front and center. Each choir is different, as is each choir loft. Only trial and error will determine the optimum seating pattern for each voice section, and for the entire choir. But there *is* an optimum seating plan, and the director should experiment until he finds it.

Assisting the Older Singer

Singers past the age of 40 are not found in college choirs, are somewhat rare in professional choirs, but are the mainstay of church choirs. The director of the church choir must know how to get the best results from older singers.

Older church choir singers have some real advantages:

- They have good attitudes, and are steady and loyal.
- They already know a great deal of repertory.
- They are usually experienced readers.

But aging does bring physical change to the body, and to the voice in that body. Noble Cain observed that most voices reach their peak when the singer is in his mid-30's. From that age, there is a slow but inevitable loss of abilities. With aging, the voice becomes:

- Less flexible in dynamic control.
- Less reliable in pitch.
- More restricted in range.
- More easily fatigued.

In general, vocal problems associated with aging are physical, not mental. Truly, the spirit remains bright and willing, but the body and voice become weaker. Much of the undesirable voice production by older singers is the result of excessive physical effort used to compensate for diminished vocal ability. Excessive effort results in the forced tone, the wide vibrato, and the improper placement of the voice, which are typical of some older singers.

It is not a kindness to allow older singers to strain in overcoming vocal obstacles. They should be tactfully re-assigned to voice parts that are in keeping with their present abilities. The former first soprano who now hoots or screams on the top notes may be ruining your choir. Yet she may enjoy another decade of useful singing in a more comfortable second soprano part. There should be no resentment of this if the director has maintained a general policy of flexibility and adaptability.

WORKING WITH THE DIFFICULT SINGER

Correct Serious Faults Quickly

The difficult singer is one who does not fit into the choir easily. Sometimes it's the voice that doesn't adapt readily, sometimes it's a personality. In some cases, it may be both; an abrasive personality is often mirrored in a harsh voice.

As soon as the director recognizes a problem voice, he should start remedial action. One bad voice can spoil an entire choir, just as one drop of kerosene can spoil a whole kettle of soup. The other members of the choir are immediately and acutely aware of problem voices, and they rightly expect the director to take action.

Every singer is hypersensitive about his voice; all resent criticism. Yet corrections must be made. To avoid direct personal confrontation, it is sometimes best to work with an entire section. The majority of voice problems can be alleviated if the singer will do four simple things:

1. Sing more quietly.
2. Listen more carefully to others.
3. Listen intently to his own voice.
4. Consciously match his tone to the group.

The failure to listen lies at the root of many choral problems.

Where group or sectional training is not successful in correcting an individual voice problem, the director should arrange private instruction. If the abnormality still persists, he must ask the individual to leave the choir. As difficult as this may be, it is not fair to permit one individual to frustrate the efforts of the entire group.

And the longer the director tolerates a really bad voice, the greater is the resentment of the other choristers.

Living with Human Nature

Not all choir singers are saints or angels. Like other human beings, some are easily offended, critical, jealous, cantankerous, and can behave at times with inexplicable irrationality.

Humans in groups, including church choirs, seem prone to establish "pecking orders" as they vie for position, prominence, and approval. Within the group, some will set up interesting little psychological games. The choirmaster cannot expect to change human nature, nor re-shape human personality, but he should stay out of the games, either as participant or referee. Follow these guidelines:

- Be impartially fair to everyone.
- Never comment upon one singer to another.
- Don't get involved in cliques.
- Tend strictly to the music business.
- Keep everyone so busy at rehearsal that they have little time or energy for extra-musical activities.

On rare occasions, a personality problem can become so serious that the whole choir is disrupted. In such a case, the director may need to dismiss a singer from the choir. This is always a distasteful task, but it may help if one remembers:

a. The indispensable singer has not yet been born.
b. No singer is more important than a whole choir.
c. Reliance on one voice must never become dependence.

ABSENTEEISM: SCOURGE OF THE CHURCH CHOIR

Attendance Determines Accomplishment

Absenteeism is the universal scourge of the church choir. Under no circumstances can excellent performance be attained without excellent attendance at rehearsals. The director of a professional choir knows this well, demands 100% attendance at rehearsals, and is willing to pay to get it. The director of the church choir also needs 100% attendance at rehearsals. Since he is usually unable to buy this, he must do his best to win it without substantial financial rewards. It is not an easy task.

The Absentee Hurts the Whole Team

In a choir of volunteers, some absence is inevitable because of business engagements and travel, illness, or family emergencies. But a great deal of absence can be attributed to relatively frivolous causes: inclement weather, a favorite TV program, tiredness after a busy day, etc. It is this sort of absence that kills the church choir.

Choral singing is a "team sport" requiring "team players." The typical church choir reputedly has less than 25 voices. Thus, the absence of two or three people out of one voice section can have a detrimental effect on the sound of the entire choir. If there are seven sopranos, six altos, five tenors, but only two basses instead of the usual five, the sound of the entire choir is altered, not the sound of the bass section only. Like an automobile with three good wheels and one flat tire, the choir with one missing voice section isn't going very far. Remember:

- Every rehearsal is important to every singer.
- Every singer is important at every rehearsal.

Minimum Acceptable Attendance: Two out of Three

As an absolute minimum, each singer should expect to attend two out of three rehearsals. If he cannot do so, the choir will sound better without him. Better a smaller, well-prepared group than a large choir encumbered with poorly rehearsed part-timers.

Handle cases of persistent absenteeism on an individual basis. Remind the singer that he has been missed at rehearsals and await his explanation. Often, the fact that the director has shown a personal interest will encourage the singer to attend more regularly. He may just want attention.

PRACTICAL WAYS TO BUILD BETTER ATTENDANCE

Oral Roll Call Offers Advantages

Accurate attendance records are fundamental to the encouragement of regular attendance. In most church choirs, these records can be compiled by the director himself. Recording attendance takes just a few moments and provides at least a fleeting contact with each individual singer. The director can compile his records by silent observation or oral roll call.

Oral roll call does take up some valuable rehearsal time, but the advantages may make it worthwhile. Oral roll call:

- Emphasizes to the choristers the importance of attendance.
- Helps the singers to learn each other's names.
- Gives brief recognition to everyone; people do like the sound of their own names.

Ask each singer to answer "Sunday" in responding to roll call, if he intends to sing at the next service. This confirms his intention to sing as well as recording his presence at rehearsal. If he will not be able to sing on the following Sunday, he can immediately explain the reason for his expected absence. If plans do change, the singer should get word to the director or the church office.

Where the director places obvious emphasis on attendance, his singers will tend to do the same.

Interesting Music Is the Prime Attraction

The most important inducement to good attendance in the church choir is a program of interesting and worthwhile music. Music, after all, is the unique attraction of the church choir, the one thing that sets it apart from all other organizations. Where the music itself lacks appeal, other inducements and stimulants to attendance will in the end avail very little.

Each rehearsal should be a pleasant and stimulating learning experience. Singers may find it easy to stay away from choir when their music is dull or discouragingly difficult. It is the director's responsibility to make each rehearsal an exciting musical event which the singer will wish to attend. Too often, the choirmaster's own lack of interest is a root cause of poor rehearsal attendance. If he does not look forward with keen anticipation to each rehearsal, why should the choristers?

Morale—Recognition—Rewards

High morale in the choir is a pre-requisite to good attendance. The late General George Marshall once defined morale as "Pride in the organization and a belief in its purpose."

In addition to being proud of the choir, and believing in its purpose, the singer needs also to develop a sense of his personal responsibility and individual worth in the choir. A singer should never have the feeling that he is "just one of the mob." Each person should feel that he has a unique place in the choir, or a special niche in the music program.

Nearly everyone has some special talent or hobby that can be made useful in the total music program. Help each person to fulfill some special function in addition to singing in the choir. Among the possibilities:

- Sing solos.
- Sing in a descant group.
- Sing in a small ensemble at special services.
- Help with accompaniments.
- Organize and direct small ensembles.
- Play an instrument solo or in ensemble.
- Help with library work.
- Help with robe repair.
- Contact prospective choir members.
- Follow up absentees.
- Help on social committees.
- Work on publicity.
- Make posters or charts.
- Write news releases.
- Photograph choir events.
- Help with staging or transportation in special programs.
- Run electronic equipment at rehearsals.

Recognition and appreciation are among the most powerful of human motivations. Be quick to recognize extra effort. Recognition may be no more than a nod or wave, a fleeting smile or glance of encouragement in rehearsal or performance. A public "thank you," or a personal note is often appropriate and always appreciated. The director of music has many reasons to be thankful each week, and his gratitude should find ready expression.

More formal systems of recognition may also be beneficial:

- Singers with outstanding records can be named in the church bulletin periodically.
- The choir letter or yearbook can list the attendance of all singers, headed by those with the best records.
- Have a large attendance chart in the choir room.
- An annual ceremony of recognition or re-dedication can be part of a church service.

- A post-rehearsal party once each month can recognize those with perfect attendance or those with birthdays during the month.
- Send a birthday card to each choir member.

Official recognition by the church board or clergy is also welcome. Such recognition could be:

- An open letter.
- A brief visit at rehearsal or at a party.
- A reception for choir families.
- An annual choir banquet.
- Refreshments after a choral performance.
- Complimentary tickets for a concert.

One step beyond recognition is the giving of awards. These are widely used with children's choirs but have also been effective with adults. When awards are to be given, the singer must know in advance exactly what he must do to qualify. The granting of awards should never be arbitrary. Awards which have proven effective are:

- Money.
- Books or recordings.
- Tickets to concerts.
- Attendance at summer music camps.
- Attendance at a special party.
- Certificates and pins.
- Ribbon clusters on robes.
- Special stoles with choir vestments.

Signing On for Special Events

For special events or special services, it is useful to request sign-ups as a gauge to the expected attendance. This should be done about two weeks prior to the scheduled event.

A simple form will facilitate the sign-up; identify the event precisely, list each chorister's name, and ask for a definite "yes" or "no." (See Illustration 3-4.)

Christmas Services

Please plan to sing at all three services, or at least two out of the three.

Sopranos	Dec. 24 8:00 p.m.	Dec. 25 10:00 a.m.	Dec. 26 11:00 a.m.
Jane Allen			
Mary Alcott			
Faye Barnes			
Alice Carlson			
etc.			

Illustration 3-4

Follow Up Absentees; It Does Help

Attendance can definitely be improved by following up any absence of two weeks or more:

- *By mail.* Church supply houses offer stock postal cards for this purpose. Some directors feel that a personal card or note is preferable.
- *By telephone.* The director, section leader, or choir officer should make the call and report the result. In some children's choirs, calls are made to the home of each absentee immediately after roll call while the rehearsal is still in progress. Such calls are made by the secretary or choir mother.
- *In person.* Where a member's attendance has been especially erratic, a personal visit by the director or choir officer may be the best way to discover the cause of the problem.

Helping to Solve Individual Attendance Problems

Sometimes the director can help to organize solutions to individual attendance problems.

Transportation. Car pools may be a practical solution to transportation problems.

Baby-Sitting. Young families living on tight budgets may not be able to afford a babysitter each week. A cooperative sitting service may help. Many churches have nursery facilities which are used for infants during the worship services. Perhaps a responsible volunteer can be found to watch over the children of choir members while the parents rehearse nearby.

4 Improving Facilities for Church Music

EQUIPPING THE REHEARSAL ROOM

Poor Facilities Are a Needless Obstacle

A choir is only as good as its rehearsals. Poorly designed physical facilities are to be found in many churches, and these are a serious obstacle to productive rehearsals.

A church choir does not require elaborate or expensive rehearsal quarters, but the director has an obligation to see that his singers are provided with at least the essentials. Church administrations are not necessarily unwilling to provide adequate facilities; in many cases, they are simply unaware of what is needed, and why.

Rehearsing in the Choir Loft

Should the choir rehearse in the same place that it performs? Certainly every choir should spend some of its rehearsal time there. Only in this way can organ registration, or other instrumental accompaniment, be balanced with the choral tone. Only in the choir loft can experimental seating patterns be fully tested.

However, rehearsing music and performing music are two quite different functions. If the choir loft is to be used for all of the choir's rehearsals, it is likely to require some modification.

a. The acoustics in some choir lofts are so poor that singers may have great difficulty in hearing each other. This can be a most severe handicap in developing choral ensemble. Unfortunately, poor acoustics are not easily corrected, being a defect built into the design of the building. It is usually best to rehearse the choir in a more suitable place.

b. While the organ is widely used to accompany choir anthems, it is not a good instrument for choir rehearsals. A piano is much preferred because its incisive tone can more clearly delineate pitch and rhythm for the choir. If the choir must rehearse in the church choir loft, make certain that you have a piano available.

c. Lighting is often inadequate in choir lofts. Typically, illumination in churches is more ornamental than functional. You may need supplementary lighting for decent vision.

d. Some choir lofts are beneath large stained-glass windows; hot in summer, cold in winter, and always poorly ventilated. Uncomfortable singers won't learn much.

e. Even where the choir loft is satisfactory for rehearsing, it is necessary to have space for storing choir vestments and music. An additional area will be needed for assembling and warming up the choir before the worship service.

Summing up, wherever possible, the choir should have adequate rehearsal facilities apart from the choir loft.

Rehearsing in Multiple-Purpose Rooms

Not every church is able to provide a room set aside exclusively for the use of the choir. In most churches, the large rooms are designed for multiple use: church school, confirmation classes, circle meetings, etc. Nearly any large room can serve very adequately for choir rehearsal.

Basic Features of a Good Rehearsal Room

a. *Flexible seating arrangements.* Moveable chairs are preferable to any kind of stationary seating. The director should be free to experiment with various seating patterns, ranging from straight rows to circles. Platform risers in the rehearsal room usually restrict the flexibility and freedom of seating. Their use puts an undesirable distance between the director and his choir. However, if the choir has over 50 singers, risers may be the most practical solution to rehearsal seating.

b. *Chairs should aid good singing posture.* Erect posture is important to good singing. Most folding chairs do not encourage good posture; many are, in fact, quite uncomfortable. There are chairs which have been specifically designed for choral rehearsal rooms. These are relatively expensive; it is recommended that you try a few samples before you invest in them.

Low-backed stools may offer real possibilities for rehearsal room seating. They help to overcome the slumped posture so typical of chair-sitters. If the music is placed on a stand instead of hand-held, the singer has great physical freedom. He can adapt his posture to whatever effort the music calls for.

Singers should never be crowded together, whatever type of seating is used. Directors of professional choirs seem to space their singers 4 to 5 feet apart in each direction to achieve maximum tonal efficiency.

c. *A good piano is essential.* A small upright is preferred to a grand, as it accomplishes the same purpose and takes up much less space. Make sure that the piano is tuned to A = 440 so that it can be used with other instruments.

d. *Good lighting is basic.* Uniform, glare-free illumination is a prime requisite in the rehearsal room. There is no need to guess about the level of illumination. Many electric utility companies have customer service personnel who will make photometric measurements and recommend practical ways to improve the lighting in the rehearsal room. It is amazing how much more cheerful a rehearsal room can become if decorated in lighter colors and illumination brought up to recommended levels.

A word about fluorescent lighting fixtures. Many of these generate sound as well as light. This monotone hum can be most objectionable in a music room. If new fluorescent fixtures are proposed, make certain that they are a quiet type.

e. *Comfortable temperature and draft-free ventilation.* If singers are physically uncomfortable, progress in the rehearsal will be greatly retarded.

Motor-driven fans, whether for ventilation or for forced-air heating, have a detrimental effect on singing. Fans are in themselves relatively noisy, and the air turbulence which they create makes both singing and listening more difficult.

f. *High, hard-surfaced ceiling is best.* Music requires space in which to reverberate. The ceiling should be about 12 feet high, and more rather than less. The room should accommodate two to three times the number of actual singers: a choir of 25 should have enough space to seat 50 or 75.

So-called "acoustical" surfaces are usually not desirable in the choir rehearsal room. These soft, sound-absorbing materials deaden the reverberation in the room. While this is necessary in a broadcasting studio, it is usually not desirable in a rehearsal room. Much of the liveliness of choral singing comes from the reverberation of sound; it should not be dampened.

Auxiliary Teaching Tools

Teaching equipment, while not absolutely essential in the rehearsal room, can be very useful.

a. *Chalkboard.* If it is wall mounted, a chalkboard takes up no floor space. A free-standing board, while using some space, has two useful surfaces. One surface might be permanently imprinted with music-staff lines. Use the chalkboard to:

- List in sequence all music to be rehearsed.
- Write out vocal drills and exercises.
- Emphasize important announcements.
- Illustrate points of choral technique.
- Convey musical maxims, epigrams, and aphorisms.
- Outline or illustrate two-minute talks about music and musicians.

b. *Bulletin board.* A cork composition board may be mounted near the entrance to the rehearsal room. Put up fresh material each week to give the board an attractive and ever changing aspect. Singers can learn a great deal from a well-managed bulletin board. Post items such as:

- Attendance records.
- Clippings or notices of coming concerts.
- News reviews of musical programs.
- Music education posters; there are several excellent sets available.
- Pictures of composers whose works are in rehearsal.
- Cartoons about music or church.
- Local new stories about choir members.
- Sample copies of innovative music of an unusual character, or music which utilizes unusual notation.

c. *Audio equipment.* Two basic types of audio equipment can be useful in the rehearsal room:

- Sound-recording equipment.
- Sound-reproducing equipment.

Recording equipment offers great teaching potential because it lets us hear ourselves as others hear us. However, choral music is one of the most difficult forms to record satisfactorily; home-type units will seldom prove adequate. The making of good choral tapes requires sound-studio conditions and thousands of dollars worth of

,high-capacity electronic gear. While technical improvements are continuously made, the director should insist on an "on the job" demonstration before investing in any recording equipment.

Reproducing equipment is much more readily available. A component system is the best investment. Make sure that the components purchased are adapted to quadri-phonic sound reproduction.

Turntable. This must be equipped for precise manual operation. Generally, you will be playing for the choir only one excerpt from a large disc. It is important that the pickup arm be spotted without damage to the record surface.

Amplifier. It should have multiple inputs; you may wish to add a tape deck or radio receiver. The amplifier is the heart of the sound system; good quality is essential.

Speakers. These should be carefully matched to the capacity and frequency-response of the amplifier. A sound system is only as good as its poorest component. It makes no sense to buy a high-potential amplifier, only to run the sound through inadequate speakers. Most audio dealers offer "packages" of well-matched components; these are usually good values.

Audio equipment provides new teaching tools. As with all tools, their effective use must be learned. Choirs are not produced by electronic wizardry; it is the director who teaches the choir to sing. Choirs always learn best by doing, and not too much rehearsal time should be spent on anything else.

ORGANIZING THE CHORAL LIBRARY

A Good Library System Saves Time and Money

The choral library represents a very substantial investment of both time and money. A good library system will protect this investment by preventing loss and damage to the octavo, whether in use or storage. Further, a good library system will save valuable rehearsal time, which too often is wasted in circulating and retrieving music copies.

Each Singer Should Use His Own Music Folio

Numbers are basic to an effective music library system. Identify each copy of an anthem by a simple number: 1, 2, 3, 4, etc. Assign each singer a permanent music number, which is printed conspicuously on his rehearsal folio. When an anthem is distributed prior to rehearsal, the librarian puts each copy into the correspondingly numbered folio. All octavos in folio #9 will be marked #9. Each folio should be complete. Each singer should use only his own folio; "borrowing" of copies from other folios should be discouraged.

Post an accurate and current master list showing the music number assignments.

Rehearsal folios may be heavy kraft envelopes, manila wallets, press-board folders, or octavo binders especially designed for this purpose. There are two basic types of octavo binders. One holds music in place with rings, the other with elastic bands. Binders are very convenient for the singers and provide good protection for the music. They are somewhat more troublesome to the librarians, who must insert and remove the copies. Octavos to be used in binders require special reinforcement. For ring-type binders, protect the punched holes with cloth rings to prevent tearing. For use in elastic-band binders, reinforce the center fold with cloth music tape to prevent ripping at the seam.

When not in use, rehearsal folios should be stored in a cabinet with individually numbered compartments. The storage cabinet may be stationary or mobile, as convenient. Storage in numbered compartments is much preferred to storage of rehearsal folios in stacks or piles. Singers can find their own folio much more quickly, with much less damage from handling.

Folios should be distributed cafeteria-style, each chorister picking up his own as he enters the rehearsal room and putting it back as he leaves. Singers who wish to take their music home should check it out with the librarian.

In addition to the utilitarian rehearsal folios, many church choirs use a more decorative music folder for the worship service. This usually contains only the music to be used in the service.

Receiving Newly Purchased Music

When new music is received, each copy should immediately be branded with the church choir's identifying rubber stamp:

```
Property of
FIRST CHRISTIAN CHURCH
CHOIR
Hometown Ohio
```

The identifying serial number should be added in ink; a felt-tipped pen makes very visible numbers which resist unauthorized alteration.

One copy of each new anthem should be marked "Director" and another "Accompanist."

Whenever new music is purchased, order about 20% more copies than are immediately required. There is always some attrition of octavo music, despite the best efforts of the librarians. With distressing regularity, church anthems go out of print, and replacements may later be impossible to obtain.

Distributing and Retrieving Octavos

Librarians should put the music in the rehearsal folios seven or eight weeks in advance of performance. This can be done automatically where the director publishes a Choral Music Schedule for an entire unit.

If binders are used, the librarians should insert each copy in the proper binder, rather than trust the singers to do so.

Copies should be retrieved immediately after use. No previously performed music should remain in the rehearsal folios. The librarians should check all serial numbers on the copies to make certain that none are missing. If any have not been returned, the librarians should check with the owner of the missing serial number at once. Quick follow-up will result in more recoveries than a delayed effort.

Repairing and Re-Editing Choral Scores

The librarians will need a smooth-top table and a good work light. This will facilitate their tasks of sorting, repairing, and marking the music.

Repairs. These should be made to the music before it is replaced in storage. The most frequent damage to music is ripping at the center fold. No material is superior to hinged cloth tape in preventing or repairing such damage. Cloth tape seems to endure decades of use, and almost no other material will.

Re-Editing. Most directors make at least small changes in choral arrangements. Others considerably amplify the interpretative markings to conform to their system or ideas. These markings should be inserted in the copies by the librarians rather than by the choristers. The director should give the librarians two "corrected" copies for reference.

When making revisions in the text, the librarians should first cover the printed text with typists' self-adhesive correction tape. The new text can then be printed on this tape. Changes in the musical notation may be made in black pencil or pen. Dynamics and interpretative markings can be emphasized in red pencil. Changes made in pencil have the advantage of being erasable. After all, directors are not infallible as editors, either.

Protect Music with Safe, Clean Storage

There are several practical systems for the protection of octavo music in storage.

a. *Kraft paper envelopes.* Extra-heavy, specially imprinted envelopes are offered by music supply houses for storing octavo music. These are inexpensive, but for best results should be filed in a drawer-type filing cabinet, which is not inexpensive. Storage envelopes simply piled on shelves are seldom satisfactory.

b. *Red manila expanding wallets.* Wallets cost more than envelopes, but are much more durable. They provide good protection for music and are convenient to use. Wallets, like envelopes, are best when stored in filing drawers, rather than on open shelves. A label identifying the contents can be pasted to the top edge of each wallet.

c. *Octavo filing boxes.* Boxes protect music best of all. They may be purchased from music supply houses with or without dust covers. Octavo filing boxes cost more than envelopes or wallets, but they last much longer than either. In addition, boxes can be stored, like books, on an inexpensive open shelf.

Music larger than octavo size (instrumental parts, conductor's full scores, etc.) should be stored in music shelf boxes. These are special front-opening boxes, about 11 x 15 x 3 ½ inches. Contents should be identified clearly on the label of each box. In addition, where instrumental parts are stored separately from the choral octavo, this fact should be noted on the choral octavo storage box. (See Illustration 4-1.)

```
┌─────────────────────────────┐
│    Score and instrumental   │
│    parts in Shelf Box B      │
└─────────────────────────────┘
```

Illustration 4-1

Oratorios and other bulky choral books can be packaged in strong wrapping paper, secured dust-tight with tape or twine. Books are increasingly costly and deserve good protection while in the stacks. Label the exact contents of each package.

File So You Can Find Again

For music in storage, alphabetical filing by title is suggested. In this way, any title can be quickly located.

A card catalog or master index for the church choral library is optional. The library system can function satisfactorily without it.

If a master index is kept, use a bound book rather than looseleaf or cards. Loose materials can be mislaid or accidentally destroyed, but pages in a bound book are reasonably permanent. One page can be used for each anthem, showing title, composer, publisher, voicing, date of purchase, number of copies, dates of use, etc.

Special Files for the Director and Accompanist

The "Director" and "Accompanist" copies of each anthem should not be stored with the regular choir copies. Director and accompanist should each have a separate and complete set which includes one copy of everything in the choral library. These they ought to keep at home for study, practice, or reference.

Performance Register Provides Invaluable Records

A performance register is an octavo-size sheet of paper which is kept within the "director's copy" of each anthem. This is an amplification of the sketchy "marginal notes" which some directors inscribe on their copies.

Immediately after the performance of an anthem, write on the performance register the essential facts: date, occasion, size of choir, general level of performance, who sang solos, measures that need more work, problems to correct, notes on organ registration, etc. These are most useful guideposts to the future use of the anthem.

Weeding and Pruning the Choral Library

The choir's library (and repertory) should grow continuously through the addition of new music. But it also needs periodic weeding and pruning. Fashions in church music do change; yesterday's gems become tomorrow's junk. Each succeeding director adds at least a few new errors to the choir's repertory. When a piece of music has obviously outlived its time, it deserves dignified burial.

Once each year, the director should consider each title in the library, and remove from the stacks any moribund music. The librarians should carefully wrap this, label it clearly, and inter it in dead storage.

<u>Do Not Destroy!</u>

Musical fashions keep changing. Cycles recur. A generation or two hence, some bright young director, who has heard of Horatio Parker, Dudley Buck, and Harry Rowe Shelley, not as the most popular anthem composers of their day, but only as the teachers of Charles Ives, may uncover in your church basement a trove of their neglected musical treasures! Were not J.S. Bach and Antonio Vivaldi re-discovered in a similar way?

A Word About Loaning or Borrowing Music

Don't!

ROBES, WARDROBE, AND ROBE CARE

Robes Affect Appearance, but not Sound

Choir robes assure that all singers will be properly attired for participation in the worship service. Robes subdue the human tendency toward competitive and ostentatious dress. Robes give the choir a more organized appearance. They are said to be good for choir morale and give the singer a sense of "belonging" to an elite group.

But robes have no effect on the sound of a choir. Vestments are not essential to the performance of beautiful music in church.

Identify Robes by Number and Name

The manufacturer's label usually gives the robe length or size. In addition, each robe should have a serial number sewn in as permanent identification. A cloth tape with the current user's name may also be sewn in.

Robes should be stored on hangers. Hangers should be kept on individual hooks or in slots, each with its correct identifying number. In addition, a plastic-tape label with the user's name should be placed above each hanger slot. The use of both name and number will help to avoid confusion when everyone is trying to get his robe at one time.

A master list, with all robe assignments, should be posted near the robe storage area.

Providing Access, Light, and a Mirror

Where space in the choir room permits, a robe closet can be built along one entire wall. Accordion-fold doors protect robes when not in use, and can be pushed completely out of the way, allowing access to the full width of the closet.

Where space within the choir room is limited, robes can be distributed outside of the room by using a caster-mounted rack.

Be sure that there is good illumination in the robing area. Singers may find it difficult to locate their robes in a dark, dingy closet.

A full-length mirror is a useful piece of choir-room equipment. Ladies, especially, seem to appreciate the chance for that last quick checkup on appearance.

Choristers Should Report Needed Repairs Promptly

To advise the robe mother of needed repairs, the singer can impale a note on the robe hanger, describing exactly what needs fixing. Repairs should be made in the week following the note. Most repairs are very minor: loose snaps, tiny snags, and the like. Needle and thread should be kept right in the choir room.

Check Robe Condition Regularly

High morale in a choir is made up of many small details. It is hard for a singer to believe that he belongs to a first-class organization if he is asked to wear a robe that is soiled, shabby, or ill-fitting. Slovenly vestments bespeak slovenly management. The director cannot allow such an impression to spread among his singers. Personally check the robes once or twice a season.

Clean the Robes on a Regular Schedule

White collars on robes need laundering at least once a month and sometimes more often. In some choirs, singers themselves are responsible for this. Affluent choirs may periodically send the whole batch to the laundry. In this case, a double supply of collars must be available, as laundry delays may prevent the return of the collars for the next service.

White cottas soil quickly and are perhaps less popular than in past years for this reason. Robes, regardless of color, should be cleaned at least twice a year.

Safeguarding Choir Members' Clothing and Purses

Because church buildings are typically open and easily accessible, some congregations are perennially troubled with sneak-thieves. Choir members are frequently the victims, as purses and clothing left unattended in the choir room are tempting targets. It is wise to institute a security system before losses of money and personal items occur.

Since ladies do not usually carry their handbags or purses into the worship service, members should be advised to leave no valuables or substantial sums of money therein.

Where practical, lock up the choir room while the choir is at worship. At the least, provide a cabinet or closet where purses and personal items such as furs can be locked up during the service.

It will help to forestall theft if the building custodian or some of the ushers make periodic checks of the choir room and adjacent hallways during the service.

IDENTIFYING AND CORRECTING ACOUSTICAL PROBLEMS

Most Choirs Are Handicapped by Poor Acoustics

Among the most serious problems of the typical church choir are the acoustic deficiencies of the typical church edifice. The great majority of churches pose acoustical difficulties. These may include:

- A poorly located choir loft.
- Unsatisfactory location of organ pipes or console, or both.
- Under-balcony or around-corner seating areas that are acoustically isolated.
- Flutter-echo and uncontrolled reverberation that blunt choral diction.
- Sound-absorbent ceilings and floors in performing areas.
- Erratic electronic amplification that distorts musical performance.

Typically, the Director Is the Last to Know

The tragedy of acoustic problems is that the director of music is all-too-often blithely unaware of their existence. There is a very great difference between the direct choral sound heard by the director standing in front of his choir and the reverberated sound which reaches the ears of the congregation. A listener may assume that he cannot understand the words of the anthem because the singers' diction is weak or poorly timed. But it may in fact be the poor acoustics in the auditorium that blur the clarity of the words. The sopranos may be blamed as overaggressive, when the real culprit may be the amplification system.

Such problems are not apparent from the director's vantage point. As a result, serious situations can run on for months or years without his knowledge.

It is safe to assume that there are some acoustical problems in every auditorium; they must be acknowledged before they can be solved. The sound of your choir, as heard by the congregation, is completely at the mercy of these acoustics. The director must control the acoustics to the best of his ability, for they, in the end, control the sound of his music.

The director need not be an acoustical engineer, but he should be keenly aware of what the building is doing to the sound of his choir.

Do Church Builders Really Care?

Correct acoustic principles were very well understood by the ancient Greek builders prior to 500 B.C. Their intelligent application of these principles determined the design of the theaters which they built throughout the Hellenic world. Reportedly some of these theaters are still so acoustically efficient that a person speaking on stage can be heard by an audience of thousands without any assisting amplification. By contrast, in some modern church buildings, seating only a few hundred persons, the preacher cannot be understood without electronic amplification. Why is this?

Generally, churches simply are not designed for acoustic purposes. European churches and cathedrals, and their American imitations, were conceived mainly as monuments or mausoleums. Attention and expense were, and still are, lavished upon visual symbolism and aesthetic adornment. Little attention has been given to the acoustic consequences of the building design.

The basic plan of many church buildings is derived from patterns originating in medieval times. In those remote days, it was considered neither necessary nor desirable for common folk to hear or see what transpired in the worship service. Religious exercises were conducted by and largely for those belonging to religious orders. These elite occupied the places in church near the altar and chancel, while the laity were actually fenced away from these sacred precincts.

In Byzantine churches, ornate screens were erected in front of the altar, specifically to prevent significant portions of the Holy Liturgy from being witnessed by lay folk. Thus, in pre-Reformation times, acoustics in the church sanctuary were of no importance in its design. Such is the tyranny of tradition that church-builders still copy these medieval models, and continue to perpetrate ancient acoustical errors as if the status of the laity had not changed in the past 600 years.

Perhaps the most persistent and annoying of these antiquated errors is the divided choir loft. In the medieval church, the divided choir was a functional musical arrangement, well-suited to the antiphonal chanting of psalms or liturgical responses. But in the present day, "deaconi et cantori" no longer toss the psalm back and forth. There is no remaining liturgical justification for the divided choir loft. Yet it persists, in church after church, imposing serious if not insuperable handicaps on modern musicians. In most divided choirs—

- The singers cannot see their director clearly.
- They often cannot hear each other distinctly.
- Their tone is directed away from the congregation—a fatal failing.

Directors of many touring college and professional choirs flatly refuse to let their choirs perform in a divided choir loft. Such choirs put a tremendous effort into the production of excellent choral music. Directors rightly refuse to have their work sabotaged by an acoustical absurdity. Touring choirs carry along their own sound stage: platform risers and an acoustical shell. They set up their stage in the one best place for the performance of choral music: front and center in the auditorium. Would that the resident choir enjoyed such acoustic advantages!

Elementary Acoustics for Choir Directors

Three basic facts about sound have a direct bearing upon the acoustic problems in church auditoriums:

a. Sound-energy travels only in straight lines, like light.
b. Smooth, solid surfaces reverberate (reflect) sound-energy quite efficiently.
c. Soft, porous surfaces absorb sound-energy.

Each of these principles has important practical implications in church music.

Sound-Energy Travels Only in Straight Lines. Like a beam of light (another form of energy) sound-energy cannot be "bent" around a corner. Sound-energy goes around a corner only by being reverberated (reflected) or bounced around it. And, as in the case of a bouncing rubber ball, some of the energy is lost at each "bounce" or reverberation. Further, each reflective surface sends the sound along at a new reflective angle. Sound-energy keeps reverberating in a building until its energy is totally dissipated, usually within a few seconds.

Because sound travels only in straight lines, true, direct choral sound is heard only when choir and congregation are face to face. But this scientific truth has been often thrust aside in favor of a notion that choirs should somehow be heard, but not seen. Thus we find church choirs turned away from the congregation at 90 degrees, or tucked back into transepts where they can neither be seen nor heard very well. Others are concealed behind screens, which effectively baffle the sound. Still other choirs sing from a dark recess under the balcony, or from a lofty perch near the ceiling at the rear of the nave. The congregation listening to a poorly located choir hears only a reflection of the sound, or an electronic image of the sound, but never the live and direct choral sound.

Smooth, Solid Surfaces Reverberate Sound. A hard floor directly in front of the choir will provide excellent natural reinforcement (amplification) to choral sound, very much as voices carry clearly across a pond of still water. Sound can also be reinforced by a properly engineered acoustical shell behind and above the choir. Controlled reverberation gives music a very "live" sound. Excessively prolonged reverberation occurs in some churches with smooth stone interiors. Overlong reverberation jams the listeners' ears with a mix of direct sound and reverberant sound, neither of which will be clearly distinguishable.

Soft, Porous Surfaces Absorb Sound. A carpeted floor in front of the choir noticeably dampens choral brilliance. A church filled with people is much less reverberant than an empty church; soft clothing and hairy heads absorb a lot of sound-energy. When the auditorium is filled, it may be very difficult for sound to reach those seated at the rear. The high ceiling of a church usually serves admirably as a distributor of choral sound throughout the building. However, if the ceiling is covered with any sort of fuzzy substance (usually applied in the hope of obtaining acoustical improvement), the ceiling may simply deaden the sound by absorbing energy instead of reflecting it.

Visible Symptoms of Acoustic Ills

The director should suspect the existence of acoustical problems if he observes any of the following circumstances in his auditorium.

a. If the church building is cruciform, the nave and transepts act acoustically as separate rooms. A choir singing in the transepts is heard in the nave only by reverberation.

b. An interior dome or vault almost certainly will focus sound-energy in an uneven pattern, resulting in "hot spots" and dead corners.

c. Screens, drapes, heavy ornamental railings, or carpeting in the performing area are formidable sound barriers.

d. All singers and instruments, including the organ pipes, should be within a 40-foot radius. Aural coordination is otherwise very difficult.

e. The most efficient choir loft is slightly wider than its depth. Next best is a square loft. A wide, shallow loft makes for difficult singing, as choristers cannot hear each other well. A divided choir loft is an anathema, truly an "ecclesiastical curse."

f. Eye contact between singers and conductor should be unobstructed; no mirrors, no sidewise glances, no peeping around corners. Likewise for communication between director and accompanist.

g. If the sidewalls of the auditorium are flat and parallel, or the ceiling and floor flat and parallel, most of the sound will be trapped in a "flutter echo" before it reaches the rear of the nave.

h. Expect trouble if electronic amplification is used. Microphones placed for the preacher, liturgist, or reader often inadvertently pick up and amplify certain instruments or voices in the choir. A good rule: turn off all microphones which are not in actual use.

i. If the ceiling has been covered with a sound-absorbing material, hearing will be difficult at the rear of the nave.

j. Choir risers should be high enough to raise each row of singers completely above the heads of those in front, else much of the sound will be absorbed by the singers' hair-dos.

k. Deep under-balcony seating is a serious acoustical problem. Without loudspeakers, those seated under the balcony can hear almost nothing. In the hymns, they cannot hear the organ; they hear only themselves and consequently are sometimes completely unsynchronized with the singing of the main body of the congregation.

Tradition May Impede Correction

It is one thing to discover acoustical problems in a church; it is quite another to solve them. The dead hand of tradition is often the most formidable obstacle.

The first step is to convince the church administration of the reality of the problem; no action will be forthcoming until this is done. It is sometimes necessary to employ an outside consulting acoustical engineer. Generally, such consultants do not sell products; they simply make recommendations which the client can follow or ignore as he wishes. But, armed with a consultant's recommendations, plus unlimited persistence and patience, the director may eventually see some of the most glaring acoustic ills corrected.

Electronics Provide a Palliative, Seldom a Cure

Many acoustical ills are rooted in the basically faulty design of the building. These may be difficult to cure completely. In such cases, electronic amplification may offer the most practical palliative, if not a cure. However, there are some important qualifications.

a. An adequate amplification system is not inexpensive. The cost will be thousands, not hundreds of dollars.

b. Amplification is not a "handyman" project. Before spending money on equipment, employ experienced engineers to custom-design the system.

c. Electronic amplification is usually successful in solving only one acoustical problem: the distribution of speech. Regardless of cost, amplifiers seldom work well with choral singing.

d. Many sound engineers now avoid the old concept of stringing loudspeakers along the side of the nave. Modern installations use a carefully engineered array of speakers at the front of the church. Individual speakers in this array direct the sound towards each area of the nave.

An operator should be in attendance whenever the sound system is in use. He should turn off all microphones that are not in actual use. He should monitor and adjust the level of sound. He should guard against screeching feedback. He should make certain that microphones are not picking up inadvertent and unwanted background sound.

INSTRUMENTAL ACCOMPANIMENT FOR THE CHOIR

The Organ: Companion, Crutch, or Competitor?

Because choral music in church is so frequently accompanied on the organ, it might be surmised that the pipe organ is the best possible instrument for this purpose. But is it?

Much of the tone produced by organ pipes falls within the same aural range as the human voice. Thus, voices-cum-organ tend to be literally "monotonous"—lacking in tonal contrast and variety. Perhaps it is because of this innate limitation of sound that great composers have seldom written for chorus and organ combined.

There are many masterworks for chorus. There are many masterworks for organ. But how many masterworks have been composed for chorus and organ?

Pipe organs are widely used in churches for reasons that are practical rather than aesthetic.

The Pipe Organ Is a Labor-Saving Device. One player, using two hands and two feet can displace a whole band of musicians playing individual instruments. And by using head and face, he can some-times lead the choir in the bargain.

The Pipe Organ Is the Loudest Instrument Generally Available. A properly designed pipe organ will definitely be heard, even in the largest cathedral. It is perhaps the only instrument that can not only "support" but actually overwhelm a church full of parishioners singing at their lustiest.

"King of Instruments" or Your Obedient Servant?

A large share of the problems choral directors experience with pipe organs stems from the fact that many of these instruments have been designed and installed primarily as solo performers. Builders proudly describe their pipe organs as the "King of Instruments," and many of these regal entities do not adapt readily to humbler ancillary roles, such as playing accompaniments for choir and congregation. Designed for brilliance in solo performance, some organs seem to lack the light, supportive stops that are so desirable for choral accompaniments.

Further, a large percentage of pipe organs are poorly located for use with the choir. Pipes are too far from the singers for effective ensemble. The console is often placed where the organist can neither see the conductor clearly nor hear the effect of his own playing.

Problems in using solo-type pipe organs are so prevalent that some directors of professional touring choirs go to great lengths to avoid using them. Roger Wagner designed a pipe organ specifically to accompany his chorale on tour. At each concert, this portable organ was set up in an acoustically correct location, even where there was a large permanent organ. Dr. Hugh Ross, director of the famous Schola Cantorum, and one of the most knowledgeable of choral conductors, writes: "I actually prefer a good portable electronic model to one of the grandiose 100-stop instruments, simply because it will give you what the music calls for, and can be moved to the most convenient position with very little trouble."[1]

Problems with Pipe Organs

Pipe organs regularly require mechanical service and tuning. These professional services are costly, and as a result many church organs simply do not get the attention they deserve. A chronically out-of-tune organ can have a most unfortunate effect on the singing of both the choir and the congregation.

Even many well-maintained organs have recurrent pitch problems. Organ pitch is affected by temperature and humidity. Cold contracts the pipes, causing them to go sharp. Heat expands the pipes, causing them to go flat. These deviations in pitch are less serious if the whole instrument is uniformly affected. But often different sections of the instrument have been installed in different temperature zones, so that some pipes are more affected than others, and the instrument goes out of tune with itself.

Other problems with pipe organs occur because of the obdurate fact that sound travels at about 1,120 feet per second. Thus, in a very large cathedral or auditorium, it is almost impossible to coordinate the congregational singing. Those seated at a distance from the organ hear the instrument somewhat later than those seated

---

[1] Neidig and Jennings: *Choral Director's Guide,* p. 280. Parker Publishing Co., Inc., West Nyack, New York, 1967.

near it, and all sing accordingly. Each group may be right, but together they sound wrong.

The Practical, Percussive Pianoforte

For choral rehearsals, the pianoforte is an almost ideal instrument. It is percussive enough to delineate pitch and rhythm clearly. It is durable, generally holds its tuning well, and requires a minimum of maintenance.

Pianos should be kept away from radiators or heating vents, as the excessive dehydration from these sources may cause the sounding-board to crack, or, at the least, will put the instrument out of tune.

The piano, in performance, is not well suited to doubling the voices in music which should be sung "a cappella." It is more acceptable where the composer has provided a fluent and independent accompaniment.

Harpsichords: Delightful but Delicate

The world around, singing is accompanied by plucked, stringed instruments. Lyres, harps, psalteries, along with their cousins in the guitar family (zithers, sitars, kotos, balalaikas, etc.), are almost universally used to complement the human voice, and have apparently been so used since the dawn of man-made music.

Voices and plucked strings make aesthetic sense; such instruments beautifully enhance the effect of singing. Unlike a wind instrument, such as the organ, a plucked string will not compete against, nor cover up even a light singing tone. A singer is neither tempted nor goaded into trying to outshout the harp.

Lyres and harps are not widely available for church use at the present time. Guitars, of course, are being increasingly used in church music. They are, however, not technically capable of accompanying many of the serious musical forms. The harpsichord, however, is quite capable of doing so. It combines the technical facility of keyboard instruments with the light, bright sound of the plucked string. Voices and harpsichord form a delightful musical combination.

With the ascendency of the pianoforte in the 19th and 20th centuries, harpsichords were eclipsed and technical improvements almost ceased. As a result, many "modern" harpsichords are consciously designed and constructed on 18th century principles. Many are as delicate as they are delightful. A few changes have been made; with some regret, hobbyist-builders have become reconciled to plastic plectra to replace the authentic goose- and crow-quills of yesteryear. But in major respects, the harpsichord of today may be little changed from its ancestor of 200 years ago. As a consequence, the present-day harpsichordist, just like J.S. Bach, can expect to:

- Spend 15 to 20 minutes tuning the instrument each time he plays it or moves it.
- Coddle the instrument through every change of temperature and humidity.
- Replace broken strings with annoying frequency.
- Tinker periodically with a quaintly archaic key mechanism.

Such mechanical crochets may actually endear the harpsichord to the truly dedicated hobbyist. But the church musician, with performance deadlines to meet, may be pardoned if he longs for the day when contemporary technology will produce a harpsichord as durable and reliable as, for example, a piano.

The light, silvery tone of the harpsichord does not carry strongly in a large church with a large choir. Harpsichords can, however, be readily amplified with guitar-type electronic equipment. Amplification must be guided by restraint and good taste, else the distinctive beauty of the tone may be distorted beyond recognition.

Some contemporary harpsichords now have amplification built in. And an excellent analog of harpsichord tone is now being produced electronically.

Electronic Instruments: Past, Present, Future

A large number of church choirs are already accompanied on electronic organs, which have been the principal electro-musical instruments of the past. Rapid technological improvement and innovation in the creation of electronic sound have opened to the director of church music new and exciting musical possibilities. The future of music may be, as Virgil Fox observes, electronic. It is evident that electronic instruments have the capacity to alter completely the traditional concepts of instrumental music and choral accompaniments in our churches.

The Past. The pioneer among electro-musical instruments is the "electric organ." Early models were much criticized because they attempted, and generally failed, to reproduce the tone of the pneumatic pipe organ. Despite persistent criticism from the musical elite, electric organs won wide acceptance because they offered practical advantages, especially to the smaller congregation:

- The tone, if not truly organ-like, was useful.
- Cost and upkeep were usually less than for pipe organs.
- Much less space for installation was required, an important advantage in a small sanctuary.

It should be observed that electric organs 20 to 30 years old are now as technologically outmoded as phonographs or television receivers of the same vintage.

The Present. Modern electronic organs are vastly improved over their prototypes. Tone generation and amplification have reached the point where these instruments function well in a large auditorium.

In addition to organs, we are now seeing new forms of electro-music in church. Amplified guitars are no novelty, and tastefully used, can create some beautiful musical accompaniments and ensemble effects.

In addition to amplifying tone, a whole new class of electronic devices modulate the natural tonal character of conventional musical instruments. A clarinet, for example, can be modulated to sound very much like a cello, or an oboe, or a trumpet. Equipped with a modulator, a single instrumentalist can thus create and control a great variety of useful musical sounds.

In addition to electric organs, other electronic keyboard instruments are now available. Among these is the electronic piano/harpsichord. Some of these reproduce the harpsichord tone with startling fidelity, and can be amplified to nearly any desired volume. Robert De Cormier has used this instrument with his touring professional choir, with excellent musical effect. The piano/harpsichord may offer fine possibilities for church use, as it produces the tonal characteristics of the harpsichord without that instrument's mechanical complications.

The Future. Practical tonal "synthesizers" are now a reality, although present models will no doubt seem primitive within a few years. Two courses of development are apparent in synthesizers, both of which hold tremendous promise for the future of church music, and all music.

a. It is becoming technically possible to synthesize the sound of almost any conventional musical instrument, from tuba to piccolo.

b. Synthesizers can also create entirely new sounds, and musical effects, totally unlike the sounds of existing musical instruments.

In the past, directors of church music have had to rely on the local supply of skilled instrumental players. Players of baroque trumpets, for example, have always been in short supply. The synthesizer will make it possible for the director to have at his command tonal analogs of nearly any orchestral instrument. The player needs only modest skills to handle the keyboard.

It is thoroughly practical to incorporate synthesizers and other electronic instruments into the church music program in an evolutionary manner. Perhaps we shall see the development of ensembles, combining organ (pneumatic or electric) with electro-piano/harpsichord, percussion and electric guitar/bass. A basic ensemble of three or four players could be augmented on occasion with additional instruments. For the forward-looking church, the musical possibilities are virtually unlimited.

5 Selecting Appropriate Church Music

Music Affects Every Performer and Listener

No single factor is of greater importance in the success of the church music program than the selection of music to be performed. It is the music that largely determines the character of each worship service. For better or worse, music is likely to make a stronger impression on the churchgoer than anything else that occurs in the service.

a. *Music affects the choir.* The most immediate effect of music selections is evident in choir interest and attendance. Choristers do respond positively to music they enjoy. If they are enthusiastic about the music, they enjoy coming to rehearsals, and will work eagerly to perform it well. Good music builds good morale.

b. *Music affects the congregation.*

" . . . . .Some to church repair
Not for the doctrine, but the music there."
 Alexander Pope (1688-1744)

Church music has an important missionary and didactic function; it attracts people to the church and presents religious ideas in persuasive and memorable form. Music is part of the spiritual food which nurtures a congregation.

c. *Music affects the clergy.* The pastor is responsible for the entire service of worship. When music contributes to the service in a positive way, it is to his credit, as well as yours. And when things go badly, or when your selections arouse controversy in the congregation (as perhaps they sometimes should), the pastor will be involved.

d. *Music affects the director.* The director who is growing continually expands his knowledge of repertory. He will study innovative and experimental choral scores, most of which he would never schedule for his church choir. But, as the chief musician of the church, he ought to be fully informed in his special field and be able to introduce to the choir and congregation a wide variety of interesting music of the highest quality. The musician who feels comfortable with only one sort of church music is in a groove that will likely become a rut.

To Be Truly Beautiful, Music Must Be Appropriate

Church music ought to be beautiful music. This is not to say that it should always be pretty music. Rather, church music should be beautiful in the classic Greek sense, expressed in their word "kalos," which meant beautiful, but also good, appropriate, fitting, and graceful. Pretty, pleasant music may be very well suited for use in some church services. But merely pretty music might be quite inappropriate in a somber Holy Week service, hence would not be "beautiful." In commemorating Christ's agony on Gethsemane, or the horror of Golgatha, dissonance, while not pretty, might be more appropriate and thus more beautiful than consonant harmonies.

In his "Passion According to St. John," Handel has the crucified and dying Jesus singing "I thirst!" four times, with the bel canto flourishes typical of 18th century Italian opera. Pretty it may be; beautiful it is not. Of course, Handel was only 19 when he wrote this, and learned a great deal about beauty before he composed "The Messiah" at age 57.

True beauty depends only partly upon qualities intrinsic in the music; it also depends upon the circumstances in which the music is presented. To be truly beautiful, church music must be appropriate in three ways.

Appropriate to the choir, suitable to its size and sonority, its musical ability and comprehension.

Appropriate to the worship service, in harmony with the theme and emotional tone of the service, whether festive or somber.

Appropriate to the congregation, communicating in a musical language understandable to them, in keeping with congregational cultural patterns and worship traditions.

Unsuitable Music Is the Root of Many Choir Problems

A program of dull, dreary anthems is directly responsible for the apathy and ennui that too often mark the weekly rehearsal of the church choir. A director who himself is bored with his music, or holds much of it in contempt, is not likely to conduct an inspiring rehearsal. A condescending attitude towards the music cannot be concealed by a conductor. Indifference is easily detected, and is highly contagious, quickly infecting a whole choir. Prevention is the only remedy: *schedule for your choir only that music for which you feel a genuine enthusiasm.*

Beautiful music is invariably emotional music; it evokes an emotional response. Emotion energizes; it's what "turns us on." When a church choir and its director are emotionally involved with their music, nearly all things are possible.

CHURCH MUSIC AS A SPECIAL FORM OF RELIGIOUS MUSIC

Music, by Nature, Is Neither Sacred nor Christian

There is no inherently "sacred" music.

In Christian theology, God alone is holy and worthy of worship. Material objects, including art and music, are never in themselves to be worshipped. The worship of "things" for their own sake is idolatry. It is true that certain kinds of music (as well as other art forms) through ancient custom and usage in worship seem to become "sacred" or "holy." Such sacredness or holiness, however, in no way derives from the nature of the music itself, but solely from its association with Divine worship. Most religions and cultures have music which is "sacred" in this sense.

The world over, vastly different kinds of music are used in religious services; hence, there is the greatest diversity in that which is thought to be "sacred" music. The musical distance between Gregorian chant and the Missa Luba is enormous. But regardless of the diverse character of religious music, if it is successful in its own time and place in turning men's thoughts towards God, it is by them deemed to be "sacred music." Thus, what is to be called "sacred" depends entirely upon subjective judgement by the worshipper; there is no universal quality nor character in music itself which makes it sacred. If, when he hears it, the music leads the believer to think of God, that music is to him "sacred."

There is no inherently "Christian" music.

Christianity is an ecumenical faith. Adherents are to be found in the most diverse cultures the world over. In each of these cultures, Christians have developed forms of music for use in their religious exercises. An astonishing variety of music can thus properly be termed "Christian."

To the Armenian, the elaborately involuted cantillation "Khorhoort Khorin" is Christian music. To the Congolese, the pulsing jungle-drum rhythm of the Missa Luba is Christian music. To some Caucasian Christians, Palestrina's "Missa Pappae Marcelli" is the very epitome of Christian music. Others would choose Bach's "Passion According to St. Matthew" or Handel's "Messiah" as ideal Christian music. Yet millions of others greatly prefer "Onward Christian Soldiers," "My God and I," "When the Saints Come Marching In," or "Jesus Christ, Superstar." Since all of this music is somewhere meaningful in Christian worship, all can rightly be termed "Christian music." For Christian music is whatever kind of music is customarily used in Christian worship.

While Christianity is ecumenical, its adherents can sometimes seem narrowly parochial. Cultural groups among Christians have characteristically proclaimed their special kind of music to be the "true Christian music," implying that the music of other groups is inferior, if not downright heretical or sacrilegious. But perhaps a more truly ecumenical day is dawning. When Pope Paul VI visited the Island of Sardinia, he was greeted by a choir singing not the traditional "Tu Es Petrus" but "When the Saints Come Marching In"—in Italian, of course. His Holiness appeared to be delighted.

Religious Music vs. Church Music

A distinction should be made between religious music and church music. All church music ought to be religious, but not all religious music is suitable for use in the church service.

Many of the great masterworks of religious music are in themselves artistic entities. Their creators conceived them on a scale that precludes their inclusion within a normal service of worship. The great religious oratorios, the great settings of the mass, such as Bach's

B Minor or Bruckner's F Minor, are complete in themselves. They are sublimely religious works, but they are not church music.

Church music is religious music which fits comfortably within the framework of the worship service and can be readily performed by the musical resources normally found within the congregation.

Great Church Music: God-Expressive and Economical

To be termed "great," church music must prove its ability to speak to Christians in many ages and many places. Much great church music is distinguished by two virtues:

a. It is God-expressive rather than self-expressive.
b. It is understated rather than overstated.

In the most enduring church music, there is scarcely one superfluous note. The simplicity and economy of means which characterizes great church music beautifully illustrates the dictum of the 14th century English philosopher, William of Ockham, who wrote: "It is vain to use more to accomplish that which can be done with less." The great masters of sacred choral writing such as Vittoria, Palestrina, Lotti, Farrant, Schuetz, Bach, and Bruckner are able to express as much with four voices as other composers can with a full symphony orchestra.

Look for Beauty, Emotion, Simplicity, Strength, Integrity, Originality

In selecting music for his choir, the director should look for specific virtues.

Beauty of thought, language, and musical art. Music that is sensitive and reflective of its text. Fresh and attractive musical ideas.

Emotion. Sublime or stirring thought; ideas to which performer and listener can respond emotionally. Inspirational choral writing that gives worshippers a spiritual lift.

Simplicity. Music well within the ability of the singers. A direct communication easily understood by the congregation. Emphasis on spiritual values, not on technical complexities.

Strength. In music, as in architecture, strength derives from structure, not from bulk. In strong music, form and structure are lucid and logical. Strong music requires no tacked-on ornamentation. Avoid bombast and pomposity. Remember always that "Less is more."

Integrity. Words and music must strengthen each other. Avoid mindless repetition of text or theme. Discard music which is mere technical display. Church music is not "show biz."

Originality. Both text and music ought to be truly distinguished; some fresh insight, or a new way of illuminating an eternal truth. Seek that spark of creative genius that sets the work apart from the trite and ordinary.

Great Church Music Brings an Ageless Message

Perhaps the least important thing about church music is its age. The great composers of church music have always written not for their own time and place only, but for the whole church. The message of great church music is as pertinent to 20th century man as it was to man in the 1st, 6th, or 16th century. And while musical techniques change and expand, music remains truly a universal language, readily understood in all ages and in all places. Thus music which may be four centuries old speaks today with undiminished vitality. Age in church music simply is not an important factor. The composer of today may, in fact, be hard-pressed to create choral music that sounds as alive as that which is centuries old.

Authoritarian Standards for Church Music

Nowhere in scripture is revealed the Divine Will about music. God has left no instructions on what sort of music or musical performances He sanctions. It would thus appear that concerning music, no man can rightly claim to speak the will of God.

Nonetheless, church authorities at times have assumed the right to establish rules concerning the kind of music to be used in the church and arbitrary regulations concerning its performance. In some churches, only anthems with Scriptural texts may be used. Others have ruled that music may be sung in church only by unmarried males; females have been widely barred from participation. Many such traditions have been under attack in recent years, and regulations set aside or ignored.

Historically, most American denominations originated as missions to serve immigrants to the New World. As missions, they were financed and controlled largely by the mother churches back in Europe. Worship services were conducted in the language of the fatherland; clergy were imported from Europe or were at least trained there. The styles of church music which were familiar in the old country were highly favored. Long after attaining financial independence, many American congregations, both Catholic and Protestant, maintained a strong cultural dependence upon Europe. Leading Episcopal churches imported Anglican organists and choirmasters from England to bring the torch of enlightenment to the Colonials, as late as the 20th century.[1] Roman Catholic musicians who had been trained in Rome bore a special authority. The leading Lutheran musicians studied in Germany; their American choirs sang almost nothing but European music. In some cases these cultural tastemakers made no effort to conceal their contempt for indigenous American music.

At long last, this dependence on European culture seems to be waning. American church musicians appear less timid about setting their own musical standards; American congregations seem more ready to accept indigenous musical forms. Spirituals and gospel songs are becoming acceptable even to the major conservative denominations.[2] Increasingly, composers draw upon typical American musical idioms such as folk-song, jazz, and rock, which were spurned during the long period of European dominance.

Introducing New Musical Idioms in the Worship Service

If you plan to use experimental or possibly controversial music in the worship service, it is mandatory that you first consult with the pastor. The pastor of any church has quite enough problems without being surprised or embarrassed by the music at his Sunday morning service. If the pastor approves in advance of novel or adventurous music, you, in return, can expect his support in the event of a strong adverse reaction from some of the congregation (which almost always does occur).

In selecting music in newer idioms, insist on the same quality which you demand in more familiar styles. First and foremost is a strong, meaningful text; if the composer has nothing worthwhile to say, it matters little how cleverly he says it. The music, of whatever type, should be well crafted, and technically within the ability of the performers.

---

[1] Leopold Stokowski was brought from England in 1905 to be organist at St. Bartholomew's in New York. T. Tertius Noble was recognized as one of England's most influential church musicians when he was engaged by St. Thomas Church of New York in 1912.

[2] The Episcopal Hymnal of 1940 was perhaps the first major denominational hymnal to break the barrier. It included "Were you there when they crucified my Lord?" as one of its 600 hymns.

Unusual church music should be prepared with unusual care. In many instances, resistance to contemporary music in church may be attributed to inept performance. One must be fair to the music, and to the listener, too.

Program notes in the church bulletin are very helpful to the listener when really unusual music is to be performed. Music must be capable of speaking for itself, but a brief introduction makes things easier for the listener. Tell something about the background of the music. Advise the listener of what to expect. Explain exactly why you are performing this music. If it is new, explain why it is an improvement over the old.

Jazz, Folk, and Contemporary Music in Church

Reactions to jazz in church are largely conditioned by one's previous experience with jazz music. Older listeners may find jazz hard to accept. When they were young, they danced and romanced to a background of jazz music. With libidinous associations, they may be truly shocked that such music would be used in church.

Younger listeners usually have no such association with jazz. They may have heard jazz in the concert hall, not the dance hall, played mainly by elderly artists who have become living legends. To the young of today, those "wicked" early-20th-century dance favorites, the waltz, two-step, and fox-trot, seem as quaint and archaic as the gavotte, sarabande, and minuet. And, like these older dance forms, jazz is being transmuted into concert music.

By no means do all older church members disapprove of jazz in church. Many realize that jazz is perhaps the most distinctive and important musical form developed in America; the influence of American jazz is world-wide. They also realize that if the Christian church is to survive for another generation, it must bring its message in whatever musical dialect the young will understand and accept.

Folk music is usually less controversial than jazz, as the average listener does not have strong secular associations with most of it. In addition, most informed churchgoers are well aware that a number of their favorite hymn-tunes were once European folk-songs. There is no reason why American folk-tunes cannot be similarly adapted.

Church music has always been influenced by the developments in contemporary secular music. At present, three trends seem to be especially prominent.

Rhythm is more free; isometric measures and regular bar-lines are disappearing.

Melodies include wide or unusual intervals. In choral music, there is an increasing use of distinctive vocal effects: whispers, shouts, semi-chant, glissando, and portamento.

This widening of resources and techniques should enable the choral composer to express his ideas with greater effectiveness than ever. However, the impression persists that many composers seem more interested in exhibiting the currently fashionable techniques than they are in achieving greater expressiveness in their music. Where the style submerges the story, the purpose of church music has been lost.

Essentials: Great Text, Expressive Music, Practicality

There is no more merit in singing music just because it's new than in singing it just because it's old. Worthwhile church music, regardless of age or idiom, should be distinguished by three characteristics:

- A text with a meaningful message.
- A style of music that enhances the significance of the text.
- A degree of difficulty that your choir can handle.

SINGING SOMETHING OF SIGNIFICANCE

In the Beginning . . . The Word

A great song begins with a great text. In church music, the primary source of all texts is the Bible, the Word of God. The greatest texts are taken directly from Scripture; the remainder are closely derived from Biblical thought.

The importance of text in choral music is almost beyond calculation; nearly everything that the composer puts into the music occurs as a result of the text. And to a great extent, the text will determine what the performers and listeners will get out of the music as well.

Text Is the Distinctive Feature of Song

The one thing that distinguishes song from all other musical art is the text. Singing combines the expressive powers of both poetry and music. In the best vocal writing, words and music interact in a marvelous way to enhance the thought and meaning of both. In church music, unquestioned primacy must be granted to the poetry. For it is the text, not the music, which gives song a reason to be in the worship service. Without significant texts to sing, there would be no choirs in Christian churches.

Every Distinguished Text Is a Drama in Miniature

Church music should have something to say about the elemental meanings of human existence: living, loving, and dying. Music should reveal something of the nature of God or man. A great text is not dryly didactic, it reveals Christian truth in a dramatic and emotional way.

Expressing Christian Thought in Noble Language

Texts selected for the church choir should meet three basic criteria.

a. *Texts should be Christian and Biblical in thought.* Specifically to be avoided are legends or fables that have no foundation in Scripture. Much of the popular music for Christmas and Easter is particularly objectionable for church use. The Nativity and the Crucifixion and Resurrection of Christ are in themselves events of overwhelming magnitude. Nothing is gained by casting an aura of incredibility over these events by associating with them fanciful tales about trees, birds, and beasts that engage in pious conversation or perform supernatural feats. Humbug, however imaginative and charming, is still humbug. Whatever their merit as concert pieces, these ditties have no legitimate place in the worship service of the church.

b. *The expression of spiritual thought should be clear and direct.* The meaning of a text should be clear to all. Obscure literary references and oblique allusions are devices belonging to the arcane and occult. The purpose of church music is communication, not confusion. A text should be lucid enough to be understood at a first hearing, yet profound enough for the chorister to ponder with profit during long hours of rehearsal.

c. *Language should be lucid, dignified, and noble.* In the greatest texts, the words make a music of their own; the song seems a natural outgrowth of their inherent musicality. A good text is timeless, perhaps ancient, in age, yet eternally relevant, speaking to all generations and conditions of mankind.

Problem Texts: Translations, Archaisms, Redundance

The director should be alert to three kinds of problems which recur in church music texts: awkward translations, obscure archaisms, redundant repetition.

a. *Translations* pose a special problem for the American church musician. The great majority of fine religious music was written in a language other than English, much in German or Latin. In American churches it is seldom appropriate to sing these in the original tongue, which is understood by neither choir nor congregation. Much wonderful music must be sung in translation or not at all.

Translations are often flawed by awkward phrasing or sentence structure which is not idiomatic to English. Seldom does the translator achieve anything like the close relationship of word and music that is found in an original version. And yet, this is precisely the quality which the director should seek in the translations which he uses. An anthem text should not sound like a translation, even if it is.

b. *Archaisms* are a peculiarity of English (Anglican) choral music.

"She was may beforn and aye . . . " Some lines may be so obscure that they scarcely make sense to 20th century ears. The confession that "Jesu is mine paramour . . ." could certainly be misconstrued by the listener who understands from his dictionary that a "paramour" is an illicit lover who usurps the place of a husband or wife.

With the richness and expressiveness of modern English, the use of antique or obscure vocabulary seems an unwarranted affectation.

Similarly pretentious is the fad for setting non-liturgical Latin texts to contemporary musical idioms. Since even the Roman church now advocates the use of local vernacular, what can be the purpose in using any language which neither performers nor audience can comprehend?

c. *Redundance* can be found in nearly all schools of choral writing from the time of Handel and Bach to the present day. Typically, the redundant composer starts with enough text for about 16 bars of music, but through some compulsion, keeps repeating this same text, or fragments of it, for 16 pages. The text thus becomes merely a pretext for an exhibition of contrapuntal skill. Excessive repetition defeats the purpose of the text. As our Lord taught (Matthew 6:7), none are heard the better for their much-speaking.

Testing a Text by Reading Aloud

One of the quickest ways to appraise a text is to read it aloud, stripped of all musical adornment. A good text must have a good sound as speech before it can be made into a great song, for song is simply speech exalted. The inflection of speech becomes melody. The pace of speech determines the tempo of the song. The emphasis of speech grows into the rhythm and accent of the song.

If the director reads the text exactly as it appears in the octavo, many faults may be revealed: inane repetition, absurdly broken phrases, platitudinous pietism, threadbare clichés. If it isn't worth reading, it surely isn't worth singing.

Unfair to Pre-Empt Congregational Hymns for Choir Use

Next to Scripture itself, Christian hymnody is the richest source of church anthem texts. A hymn provides the composer with a ready-made text which already has a cachet of respectability. In hymn-tunes, arrangers find tempting melodic material, church-related, time-tested, popularly approved. Anthems based on hymns and hymn-tunes are widely regarded as sure commercial successes by arrangers, publishers, and church choir directors.

The use of *unfamiliar* hymns and *unfamiliar* hymn-tunes in this way is to be commended. Hundreds of thousands of Christian hymns have been written over the centuries, and present-day hymnals can at best contain only a minute fraction of this accumulated musical wealth. Many marvelous hymns would be lost or forgotten were they not preserved in anthem form and sung by church choirs.

However, the use of the congregation's familiar hymns as anthem material is to be condemned. There are countless thousands of fine anthems available to the choir, if the director will bestir himself to find them. But the average congregation can sing fewer than a hundred hymns, and all-too-often the choir that fattens its repertory on a diet of these congregational favorites pre-empts the very choicest.

Hymns are the principal music still left to the congregation in the worship service. Popular hymnody should be forbidden fruit to the choir. When the director feels that he must pre-empt a familiar hymn, at the least, he should include congregational participation in the arrangement. A stirring chorale concertato, or festive hymn arrangement for congregation, choir, and instruments, can be an uplifting worship experience for all.

MUSIC SHOULD GIVE WINGS TO THE WORDS

Music and Text: Each Should Strengthen the Other

Choral music is invariably program music. The "program" is, of course, the text.

In well-written choral music, words and music are joined as partners in an ideal marriage; together they attain greater fulfillment than either could alone. Music should give wings to words, empowering them to soar to heights which words merely spoken could never reach.

In the most sublime of choral writing, the music is much more than a vehicle for conveying the text. In works such as the B Minor Mass, Bach meant the music to be his personal commentary, a portrayal in sound of the meaning of holiness and faith.

Skilled Composers Use Varied Choral Styles

In examining new music, the director can quickly check for two important characteristics of good choral writing:

- Variety in voicing.
- Variety in style of composing.

Four-part homophony, with the melody invariably in the soprano, must be the most unimaginative and overworked of choral clichés. If a choral composition is to hold interest for more than two minutes, it will need to show some variety. In good choral writing, the high, light trebles are played against the lower, darker male voices. Most great choral music employs all three basic choral styles: monophony (unison), polyphony, and homophony. An analysis of nearly any enduring choral work of the past 500 years will show that variety in voicing and style is an important key to its continuing success.

Look for variety in church anthems. Page after page of any one style is likely to prove wearisome.

Fetishism and Prejudice in Church Music

Nearly every denominational group has its musical fetishes, types of music that are reverenced to an unreasonable degree. Within a denominational group, music of the approved fetish type will be more highly regarded than its actual merit might warrant; thus, the Anglican bias for Tudor composers and Cathedral anthems, or the Lutheran leaning towards chorales and Kapellmeister music, so long as they are German. On the other side, we find those sophisticates who adore whatever music is in the latest fashion.

Conversely, prejudice often prevents the use of some kinds of church music. According to some, Stainer, Goss, and the other Victorian composers are to be shunned as the devil and all his works.

Choir directors have been heard to boast that they have never purchased "even one" anthem from a certain publisher whom they consider déclassé. One seminary professor advised his students to use no music of Brahms or Mendelssohn, as it was "too sensuous." With the changes of fashion, few types of church music have not at some time suffered the neglect, ridicule, or ostracism of the ecclesiastical tastemakers.

If the director is to do more than "follow the leader," he must develop his own standards of excellence and be secure in his own taste. No outside authority should know better than you what kind of music your choir is able to sing well, and what type of music speaks to the congregation which you serve.

Is Instrumental Accompaniment Really Necessary?

Keyboard accompaniments to choral music are of three types.

a. *Reduction of the choral score.* This is for teaching and rehearsal only. Except in emergencies, the choir should prepare to perform all such music without instrumental accompaniment.

b. *Reduction of the instrumental score.* Choruses from major choral masterworks are often published in octavo form. The original versions almost invariably were scored for orchestral accompaniment. The keyboard part which appears in the octavo is a pallid substitute for the instruments which the composer envisioned; it may be better than nothing, but not by much. Use an orchestra wherever possible. Many of the keyboard reductions of orchestral scores are not idiomatic to the organ, and require re-editing to be practical on that instrument.

c. *Independent keyboard accompaniment.* In some anthems, the composer has provided an organ part which supports and complements the voices. A good organ part should give clear leads and cues to the voices, provide interesting tonal contrasts, and show the choir off to very best advantage.[3]

Additional Instruments Increase Interest and Impact

Increasingly, composers and arrangers call for instruments other than organ in church anthem accompaniments. The use of instruments brings a fresh sound, and sometimes genuine excitement, into the worship music.

---

[3] An example of an excellent original organ accompaniment may be seen in Thomas Matthews', *The Lord Is My Shepherd,* H. T. Fitzsimons, 2137.

In considering special instrumental accompaniments, the director should be alert for some recurrent problems.

a. *Too difficult.* Most of the players available for church performances are students or amateurs, while many of the instrumental parts have been conceived for professionals. Learn firsthand what your players can reliably handle, and stay well within their limits.

b. *Parts not properly transposed.* Especially in foreign editions, instrumental parts are sometimes published in a transposition which is not familiar to American music students. Few amateurs are really adept at transposing at sight. Provide parts in the American norm for the instrument: trumpets and clarinets in Bb, French horns in F, etc.

c. *Impossible page-turns.* Instrumental parts printed as part of a choral score are almost always awkward, and often simply unplayable. Singers can turn pages anytime, but an instrumentalist with both hands busy cannot. Sometimes the instrumentalist can solve the problem by using two copies of the octavo, but it may be necessary to paste up a special instrumental part by cutting several octavo copies and mounting the instrumental parts on a large single card.

d. *Impractical instrumentation.* Arrangements sometimes call for tympani, celeste, harps, or other instruments which may not be readily available to the church. Substitutes may be quite acceptable: vibraharp for celeste or harp; cello for bassoon; flute for oboe; etc. But if reasonable substitutions cannot be made, it is best not to attempt the music.

THE BEST MUSIC IS THE MUSIC
THAT BEST FITS YOUR CHOIR

Intentions, Pretensions, and Realities

Samuel Johnson once observed that "The road to Hell is paved with good intentions." And these same good intentions burden, if not bury, a number of church music programs. A director must, of course, have good musical intentions. But unless he also has good sense, the best of intentions leads to the worst of performances. To what avail does a director schedule sublime music if the choir can't sing it or lacks time to prepare it?

Be keenly aware of the limitations of your choir in matters of technique and time for rehearsal. Resist any temptation to go beyond these limits. This does not mean that quality of music need be sacrificed. The real challenge to the choir should be the challenge of excellence in the performance of music within its means.

It's *your* choir; show it off, don't show it up.

Building a Repertory of Enduring Value

In buying new music, remember that you are building a repertory for performance, not assembling a library to impress your peers. Music purchased should have enduring values, so that once learned, it can be used year after year on an appropriate Sunday. An anthem that can't be repeated once a year probably isn't worth learning in the first place.

Be especially careful in buying music for Christmas and Easter. Some texts are appropriate for only one specific service: Christmas Eve, Easter Day, Good Friday. But other texts, perhaps of equal merit, could be used at any service throughout the Christmas season, or Easter season, or any time during Lent. It is efficient and economical to build the choir's repertory by adding new music that has a wide range of applicability.

HOW AND WHERE TO FIND SUITABLE CHURCH MUSIC

Expect One in 100 to Be Right for You

It has been estimated that about 1,500 new choral works are published in America each year. It is perhaps impossible to become familiar with such a prodigious output, but the church choir director should make some effort to do so.

Dr. Joseph Clokey once wrote that he was pleased if he found one or two useful anthems out of every 100 he examined. Dr. F. Melius Christiansen reported that after studying some 2,000 choral works, he found that 50 were acceptable, but that only six were truly outstanding.

Good music is seldom found by chance. For consistent success in discovering superior music, an organized and sustained prospecting effort is required. The search for new choral repertory is much too important to be left to chance. Time and effort must be expended regularly for consistent results.

Music Discoveries Are Unpredictable

No composer and no publisher has a monopoly on all of the good choral music. Smaller publishers are sometimes more adventurous and enterprising than some of the giants. The director must regularly check the publications from all houses, large and small, domestic and foreign.

Scanning Music Dealers' Collections

One of the most productive sources of good church choir music is the reference file of a large music dealer. Nowhere else can one examine so many octavos in so short a time. But the very abundance of anthems, numbering in the thousands of titles, requires an organized plan of attack.

a. *Know precisely the kind of music you need.* Make up a "shopping list," showing the occasions for which new music is needed: Thanksgiving, Reformation, Communion, etc. If you have instruments available for accompaniment, list exactly what these are.

b. *Use "knockout" qualifications.* Eliminate unsuitable music instantly. The text provides a sure and quick "knockout." This can be read in a few seconds of time; if it doesn't qualify, discard it at once and go on to the next title. If the text is acceptable, look for musical knockouts: extreme range; overly florid, awkward melodic lines; melodies too similar to existing repertory; etc. If you want SATB music, waste no time on the SAB, SSAATTBB, or other unsuitable voicings.

c. *Buy a single copy only.* If the music impresses you favorably at the dealer's counter, buy a single copy for additional home study. Snap judgements on first sight are always hazardous.

MUSIC FOR THE CHILDREN'S CHOIR

The children's choir does not need childish music; challenge the children both spiritually and musically.

Insist on a high standard of excellence in performance. Children sing best when they have memorized their music.

In no case should part-music be attempted until the youngsters have mastered a truly beautiful unison tone and dependable unison diction.

The vocal range in children's music should be about the same as a hymn-tune—from middle C to high E. Special training will add a few notes at either end of this span.

Instrumental accompaniment for children should be very light. Piano or organ must be used with great care, as they tend to dominate or even intimidate the children, instead of accompanying them. Ideal accompaniment is the plucked string: guitar, harp, harpsichord.

Slow, sustained music is not well suited to the child voice, viz. Palestrina's "O Bone Jesu," or "Adoremus Te." Such pieces only look easy, as they have few notes. Rhythmic folk-tunes are excellent models.

Children's choirs can do beautifully with simple mezzo arias such as Mendelssohn's "Oh Rest in the Lord" and "But the Lord Is Mindful of His Own." They can understand these texts, and can sing them very expressively.

Few can excel a children's choir in singing plainsong where suitable English texts are available. This is unison music par excellence.

Avoid treble-voice "derangements" of standard church anthems. These watered-down versions are no great musical treat for the congregation. Further, they annoy the members of the adult choir, who feel (correctly) that their repertory is thereby degraded.

Part II

How to Direct the
Church Choir

6 Programming Music for Superior Performance

PROGRAMMING IS PROFESSIONAL

Advance planning—programming—is the professional way to superior musical performance. The leading concert artists, orchestras, and opera companies work out their plans and programs a year or more in advance. They know precisely the "who, what, where, and when" of each performance.

Long-range planning gives two enormous advantages to church musicians, as well as to concert artists.

- It allows time to select a repertory that is carefully balanced throughout the season.
- It makes possible consistently superior performance through adequate preparation.

Programming is an important step towards better church music.

PROGRAMMING: KEY TO CONTROL

"Success" Is Fulfilling One's Potential

The purpose of programming is to allow the director to provide high-quality church music, well-prepared, at each worship service. Consistently good performance is a mark of professionalism.

Good performance depends upon the director's ability to match his selections to the true potential of his singers. If music is always easy and familiar, choristers will become bored with it. If it is too strange and difficult, singers become disheartened because they cannot perform it well.

The Director Cannot Escape Responsibility for Poor Performance

When music is poorly performed, the singers are seldom to be blamed. Inept performance can usually be traced to either of two causes:

a. The music is unsuited to the capacity of the performers.

b. It has not been adequately prepared in rehearsal.

Both of these causes are essentially faults in programming.

The director, not the singers, makes up the music schedule; if there are errors, they are his errors. The director, not the singers, controls the use of rehearsal time; if this is poorly utilized, it is his error, not theirs.

Never blame your singers when they have done badly. It is up to you to analyze the cause and take positive corrective action.

Counting the Cost

Jesus taught in one of his parables (Luke 14:28) that before starting a project, each man should "sit down and count the cost, whether he has enough to complete it. Otherwise, when he has laid a foundation, and is not able to finish, all who see begin to mock him, saying 'This man began to build and was not able to finish.'"

In scheduling music, "count the cost" of each selection. Do you have the voices? If there are 25 members in the choir, you can count on only 18 to 20 to be present at a typical performance. Do you have the time? It will take at least ten repetitions in rehearsal to prepare even the simplest music.

Two Minutes of Music Will Cost One Hour of Rehearsal

A typical church choir rehearses about 90 minutes each week, and sings about three minutes of music in the service. This indicates that it takes average singers about 30 minutes to prepare one minute of music. Compared to the rehearsal time spent by college or professional choirs, this is very little; perhaps totally inadequate for really superior performance.

But as a minimum time-cost, a two-minute anthem will require a full 60 minutes of rehearsal time, best if spread over a period of many weeks. A short cantata with six actual minutes of music for the chorus will require upwards of three hours of rehearsal time. These are minimum cost estimates for easy music. Difficult music will cost a great deal more time.

Programming with a Three-Unit System

For programming church music activities, units of about 14 to 18 weeks each provide a convenient format.

Unit 1: Labor Day through Christmas.
Unit 2: Epiphany through Easter Day.
Unit 3: Easter Season, Pentecost, Trinity, and Sundays after.

These units coincide with the emotional crescendos in the Christian church year. Each embraces one of the three major festivals in the Christian calendar. Within each unit, there is opportunity to use music of varying moods, from sorrow to joy.

FIRST STEPS IN UNIT PLANNING

Framework: The Calendar of Church Services

Before trying to decide *what* the choir should sing, it is necessary to determine *when* the choir will sing. The first step in programming choral music is the completion of a worksheet listing all of the services in the unit.

Many denominations publish an annual religious calendar. Your pastor will be able to provide one. Such an official calendar is a great time-saver in music planning, as it shows the significant feature of each worship service: Thanksgiving, Youth, Stewardship, Bible Sunday, Communion, First Sunday in Advent, etc. These special emphases should be noted on your worksheet, as they provide important cues to the type of music which will be appropriate for each service. (See Illustration 6-1.)

Date	Occasion	Composer	Title of Anthem
Nov. 22	Judgement Sunday		
Nov. 26 10:00 a.m.	Thanksgiving Day		
Nov. 29 *Etc.*	First in Advent. Communion		

Illustration 6-1

The Liturgical Church Year

The Liturgical churches, such as Roman Catholic, Orthodox, Episcopalian, and Lutheran, follow a traditional Christian church calendar throughout the year. In this annual cycle, each service has a pre-determined emphasis. The gospel pericope (excerpt) appointed for each Sunday provides the key to the entire service. All else in the service—Old Testament lesson, epistle, psalms, introit, gradual, hymns, anthems, motets, and instrumental voluntaries—should be in fundamental harmony with the gospel for the day. An index of these appointed texts is readily available in all liturgical churches.

Among individual congregations, there is a considerable variation in the observance of minor festivals and saints' days that are included in the official calendar. There is also a wide latitude in observing "special emphasis" days that are not included in the traditional religious calendar: Universal Bible Sunday, World Day of Prayer, Laymen's Sunday, etc. Yet these may have a most important bearing on the scheduling of music. The only safe procedure is to consult with your pastor *before* any programming of music is done. Start with a correct calendar on your worksheet.

The "Calendar of Causes"

Protestant denominations, such as Presbyterian, Methodist, and Baptist, do not officially follow the liturgical church year. The pastor and local congregational customs largely determine what is to be emphasized at each service. Denominational headquarters or a national council may suggest a "Calendar of Causes" or "Christian Concerns," as a guide to the local churches. This will usually include such observances as World Order Sunday, Christian College Sunday, Youth Sunday, Brotherhood Sunday, Rural Life Sunday, Unity Sunday, etc. Since these are simply suggestions, not edicts from a central council, it is necessary for the director to confirm the nature of each service with the pastor before he begins music programming.

Assemble Anthem Files and Reference Materials

After the schedule of services has been completed on the worksheet, actual scheduling of music can begin. Two files of anthems should be at hand:

- *Repertory file,* containing the director's copy of every anthem in the church choir library.
- *Reference file,* with single copies of anthems which the

director has studied and approved, but has not yet purchased
for the choir.

All of the music to be considered for the unit should be
contained in these two files. Of every ten selections, eight or nine
will probably come from the present repertory file; the choir can
master only a limited quantity of new music. But at least two or
three outstanding new compositions should be selected from those in
the reference file. Each unit should see some growth in the choir's
repertory.

Auxiliary reference materials will be very helpful.

Bible and Concordance. Anthem texts are often excerpts from
Scripture. It is always helpful to read the entire passage from which a
text has been extracted, viz. an entire psalm from which a few verses
have been set.

Hymnals and Commentaries. Many anthem texts are hymns.
Hymnals often contain stanzas not included in the anthem, and vice
versa; the contrasts are interesting. Commentaries give useful and
important information about the origin and history of the hymn.
This is frequently helpful in understanding and interpreting it.

Service Books. A complete compend of the Scripture used at
each service, including introit, gradual, and all lections is most useful.
A reading of these complete texts will often suggest anthem titles
that will prove to be very appropriate.

Previous Choir Performance Records. One of the most helpful
aids in programming is a record of what the choir has successfully
performed each Sunday in past seasons. This is readily available if a
good records system has been used. Otherwise, it may be had from
the church office file of past service bulletins.

PREPARING THE TENTATIVE MUSIC SCHEDULE

Unifying the Service Through Music

Music is a potent factor in setting the emotional tone of the
worship service. The mood of worship may be solemn, somber,
contemplative, joyous, or otherwise. Hymns, anthems, and instrumental voluntaries should be chosen with care to create and sustain
an emotional tone which is consistent and appropriate.

Choral music, by using words as well as tone, affects the listener
intellectually as well as emotionally; it speaks to the head as well as
to the heart. Thus it is of special importance that the anthem

programmed for each service be appropriate in its message, as well as its mood.

The late Dr. Clarence Dickinson stressed the importance of planning a coordinated and unified service. To illustrate the point, he cited the ambiguous effect of a church service in which the minister preached a stirring sermon on Luke 5:4, "Launch out into the deep!" This the choir followed with the old gospel hymn, "Pull for the shore."

In considering each possible selection for the unit program, ask and answer two questions:

- Is it *appropriate* for this service?
- Is it *practical* for my choir?

Programming Music in "Waves"

The individual anthems should not only fit each service, but also be suited to the unit as a whole. It is entirely possible to make selections that are individually excellent, but which do not add up to a practical program for the entire unit.

Volunteer singers simply cannot be driven at top speed all of the time. It is psychologically sound and technically practical to program the choir's music in emotional "waves," which peak in conjunction with the major church festivals. Begin each unit with relatively easy or familiar music, and move progressively to the more complex and musically challenging at the climax of the unit.

Dullness Is Inexcusable

Program a wide variety of musical styles. An unbroken cycle of Bach chorales, Victorian anthems, or polyphonic motets can become as tedious as a succession of gospel songs. Use some approximate percentages to insure a good mix in total unit program.

a. At least 10% but not more than 20% of the music should be new to the choir.
b. About 25% should be a cappella.
c. In about 25%, the organ accompaniment should be augmented or replaced by other instruments.
d. Texts should include both prose and poetry.
e. At least twice in each unit, music should involve the congregation: festive hymn arrangements, chorale concertatos, special liturgical settings.

Music for the Summer Unit

In many congregations, it is nearly impossible to keep the volunteer choir at an effective level through the summer vacation period.

Rather than let the choir dwindle into ineffectiveness, it might be preferable to select in advance a definite termination date for choir appearances. If the singers know when the season will end, they will usually make an effort to continue loyal attendance until that date.

When the choir is recessed, music for the worship service can be provided by soloists and small ensembles, both vocal and instrumental.

COMPLETING THE MUSIC SCHEDULE

The Music Schedule Controls Production

Programming should be completed at least three weeks prior to the first rehearsal in the new unit. Copies of the music schedule should then be printed and distributed to the choristers, music staff, and church administration. The music schedule becomes the official production schedule for the music department. Directors, soloists, and accompanists can begin their studies. The librarians can distribute the copies required for rehearsal. New music should be ordered immediately, to be on hand about eight weeks prior to the scheduled performance.

Confirm Any Revisions in Writing

Revisions in the music schedule should be held to an absolute minimum. Frequent changes in plans will greatly diminish the usefulness of any schedule. However, directors do err in programming, usually misled by their inherent optimism.

When a substitution appears to be necessary, as when ordered music is not delivered on time or an anthem is proving more difficult than anticipated, make the change as early as possible in the unit. There is little to be gained by delay, and perhaps much to be lost. Last-minute substitutions are seldom satisfactory, usually replacing one poorly prepared anthem with another.

The decision to substitute or omit an anthem should be reported in a written memo to all original recipients of the music schedule.

HYMNS ARE EVEN MORE IMPORTANT THAN ANTHEMS

In the view of some church authorities, anthems and motets are extraneous and unnecessary to worship, and could well be de-emphasized, if not eliminated from the church service. There is justification for this view where the church music administration has neglected its basic function of congregational leadership and devotes its energies solely to the rendition of showy anthems and organ solos.

In some churches, singing is the layman's only overt participation in worship. The musical leadership of the church should thus give more than intellectual assent to the importance of hymns and other congregational music. These should be as carefully chosen and correlated to the worship theme of each Sunday as the choir's music.

The director of music should further make certain that his organists and choristers understand the importance of effective leadership, and are thoroughly prepared each week to assist the congregation in the singing of hymns, responses, and psalms.

HYMNS: TRULY THE POPULAR MUSIC
OF THE CHURCH

Hymns Are for People (Not Professionals)

Hymns are the most important form of congregational music; they have been used in worship since earliest Christian times. It is of greatest importance to understand that hymns are "popular music" (people's music), intended to be sung by the ordinary churchgoer. Hymns are not the province of "experts," whether musicians or theologians.

To fulfill its purpose, a hymn must be sung by a congregation of believers. "Experts" notwithstanding, the best hymns are the hymns that people sing the best. These are usually simple, direct, and emotional. To the great disapproval of "experts" who teach that hymns ought to be objective (thee, thou), a very high percentage of the most popular hymns are subjective (I, me, we, us).

Few hymns-texts have come from the pens of distinguished litterateurs; a great many have been written by clergymen and evangelists, along with their wives and daughters. Similarly, hymn-tunes have come from great composers, but most have originated with common-folk. Hymns and hymn-tunes alike are popular music in the very truest sense—of the people, by the people, and for the people.

The hymn-tunes that people sing best are characterized by comfortable melodic intervals, conventional harmonies, obvious and repetitious rhythm. Many hymn-tunes have been worn smooth as water-pebbles through centuries of use. This causes great distress to musicologists who lament the loss of the bumpy, asymmetric rhythms and modal peculiarities which characterized the original versions.

Because hymns are by nature bland and limited in musical interest, they are not generally good vocal solo material. If a soloist sings a hymn with even a trace of dramatic operatic style, the effect can be ludicrous. Nor are hymns intended to be part-songs for the choir; the hymnal should not be considered a cut-rate substitute for true choral music.

On the other hand, hymns are perhaps the only music which can sound truly magnificent when sung by 100, 1,000, or 10,000 untrained voices. Hymns are uniquely the music of Christian common-folk, and no "experts" have the right to deprive them of their favorites under the guise of a superior wisdom.

Hymns Are the Layman's Theology

Church authorities consider hymns important because most churchgoers learn their theology from hymns. The layman sings what he believes and believes what he sings. Christian hymns are often learned at an early and impressionable age, and are repeated and remembered for a lifetime.

Hymns provide such clear and concise summations of religious doctrine that preachers in their sermons are much more likely to quote from the hymnal than from a scholarly tome of dogmatics.

Most Protestant denominations publish an official hymnal. This has been carefully censored to reflect the prevailing doctrinal views. The censorship (editing) takes two forms:

- Hymns which do not reflect acceptable theological positions are totally excluded.
- Words, phrases, lines, or entire stanzas are altered to conform with the currently dominant view.

Clergy and Musicians Should Jointly Select Hymns

In church polity, the choosing of hymns for the worship service is the prerogative of the pastor. At his discretion, he may solicit suggestions, seek assistance, or delegate the function entirely.

As a practical matter, the joint selection of hymns by the pastor and director of music has much to recommend it. Hymns chosen by consensus will reflect both the theological and musical viewpoints, which are both important in a hymn.

A great deal of time can be saved if the hymn-scheduling conference is well organized. These materials will expedite the work.

a. *Worksheets* with space for each service in the unit, similar to those used for programming choral music (p. 120).
b. *The hymnal,* plus looseleaf hymns as available.
c. *Indices to the hymnal;* these may be in the hymnal itself or published as a separate volume. Especially helpful are a liturgical index (relating the hymns to specific occasions in the church year), a topical index, and lists of hymns which are appropriate for each Sunday.
d. *Records of past selections* for similar services in former years.

In choosing hymns for congregational use, consider these factors.

Relevance. Each hymn should be appropriate to the general tone of the worship service. Seasonal hymns should be accurately programmed: no Easter hymns in Lent, no Christmas hymns in Advent.

Tunes. Select from a variety of musical styles; not all German chorales, not all Victorian tunes, nor all gospel choruses. Choose hymns in a variety of meters. Use melodies in various keys, both major and minor.

Texts. Insist that hymns be idiomatic English, especially if they have been translated. The best-loved hymns are notable for their simplicity and clarity.

Familiarity. At least two of three hymns selected should be familiar to a majority of the congregation. The singing of hymns should be an act of devotion, not a test of sight-singing ability.

The hymn-list, when complete, should be published and distributed in the same manner as the choral music schedule (p. 124).

United in Song, United in Spirit

Much of the value of hymns and responses in the worship service derives from the very act of singing together. In the act of singing, people are drawn together in an almost mystical way. When hearts are joined in Christian song, Baring-Gould's vision becomes, at least for the moment, a reality:

We are not divided, All one body we,
One in hope and doctrine, One in charity ...

In the singing of hymns, we encourage, sustain, and comfort one another in a way that goes beyond the power of spoken words. When men unite in song, they seem also to unite in purpose; we sing and we do believe that "We shall overcome ..."

A bishop whose responsibilities took him into many churches once observed that "the hymn-singing of a congregation is an almost unfailing barometer of its spiritual condition." But enthusiastic congregational singing is more than evidence of good spiritual health; spirited singing fosters and nourishes the vitality of the congregation. Whatever can be done to encourage full participation in congregational singing will have far-reaching effects on the life of the church. We sing not only because we believe, but we believe because we sing.

ENCOURAGING CONGREGATIONAL SINGING

Create a Favorable Physical Environment

a. *Seating.* People do not sing well when they are physically isolated. Unneeded sections of the nave should be roped off; ushers should seat the congregation in a reasonably compact group.

b. *Acoustics.* The effect of a sound-absorbing ceiling can be particularly depressing on congregational song (p. 86). Resonance (reverberation) greatly adds to the pleasure of singing. This is true for one man in his bath, and even more true for a church full of worshippers. Without reverberation, singing sounds muffled and lifeless.

c. *Lighting.* Many church interiors are so dimly lit that in some of the pews, people simply can't read print. Those who cannot see can hardly be expected to sing.

d. *Hymnboards.* Make certain that every churchgoer knows what hymn is to be sung, and has time to find it in the hymnal before the singing begins. Hymnboards should be large enough to be conspicuous from all parts of the nave.

Is Your Hymnal an Obstacle to Good Singing?

a. *Museum music.* Congregational music, including hymns, should reflect not only a cultural heritage, but the living culture of today's Christian. A perusal of the typical hymnal might lead to the conclusion that God can properly be praised only in musical styles which were in vogue in the Europe of 100, 400, or 800 years ago.

b. *Vocal fatigue.* Some hymns are plainly too long and too taxing to be enjoyed by the average churchgoer. Most should be limited to three or four stanzas. Some people seem to consider that omitting some of the stanzas printed in the hymnal constitutes a form of sacrilege, akin to deleting phrases of the Lord's Prayer. In truth, hymnal editors themselves have already reduced most hymns from much longer original versions. A further judicious editing to suit local conditions would not appear indefensible.

c. *Poor page layouts.* Music is easier to sing when words and notes appear in close proximity, as in the choral octavo. Unnecessary difficulties for both singers and accompanist are created by printing part of a hymn-text at the bottom of a page, or on an entirely different page. Anglican chant is particularly difficult for a congregation when printed in its traditional format; virtual memorization is required before one can truly participate. The congregation that is confused or uncertain will not sing well.

d. *Confusing organization of liturgical responses.* A widely used service book contains six versions of the Kyrie (Lord, have mercy). Unless the worshipper is absolutely certain which of these is to be sung, he cautiously (and wisely) holds back. And by the time he has found which Kyrie has just been sung, it is time to start searching for the proper setting of the Gloria in Excelsis. Such uncertainties surely diminish the vigor of congregational participation. The church bulletin may be able to help by explicitly identifying the proper response. Some bulletins, however, are even more confusing than the hymnal.

e. *Too few hymnals.* The sharing of hymnals by two or three persons is almost certain to create visual problems for some. Each churchgoer should have access to a hymnal for his individual use.

Provide Strong Leadership

The leadership of congregational song is an essential function of the choir and the organ; overall, it is their most important role in the worship service. Real improvement in congregational participation almost invariably follows an improvement in the leadership.

Choir Leadership. Voice-to-voice leading is more effective than instrument-to-voice leading. The choir must be prepared, emotionally and musically, to assume leadership in hymns, psalms, and responses; their role is a decisive one.

a. Hymns and service music should be reviewed at least briefly at each rehearsal. Never assume that the choir is familiar with hymns and responses; assure familiarity by rehearsing.

b. Sing hymns and responses in unison *only*. Unison is much more effective than part-singing in leading congregational song.

c. Teach the choir to sing hymns rhythmically, to feel and to project the heart-pulse of the song. Strong rhythm helps to keep congregational singing vital.

d. Encourage the singers to respond emotionally to music. Enthusiasm is a vital factor in effective leadership, and there can be no genuine enthusiasm without a supporting emotion. True joy in singing must be felt before it can be communicated.

Organ Leadership. Basic to all else is careful preparation. The most competent keyboard technician should each week review and rehearse the hymns and service responses.

e. Work out registrations carefully and write them down. Test new combinations during your practice period, not in the worship service.

f. Strive for solid support of the voices, not domination. Too much organ tone is counterproductive; it will discourage rather than encourage congregational effort. Seek an honest and informed opinion from others about the sound of the organ as heard in the nave.

g. Avoid sentimentalizing hymn accompaniments. It is not important for the organist to "interpret" each stanza of the hymn. It is vitally important for the organist to help the congregation to do so.

h. A hymn introduction or intonation should clearly announce the tune, set the tempo and the emotional tone, and get the congregation to singing forthwith. A full stanza to introduce an already overfamiliar hymn is but a prelude to boredom.

i. Keep the pace of the hymn moving evenly. Rubato is usually out of place in congregational song. Retarding the closing phrase of each stanza is a tedious mannerism to be avoided. Keep a strong and regular rhythmic pulse; don't let a lazy congregation drag the tempo to an ever-slower pace.

Adding Variety to Hymn-Singing

A fresh touch to a familiar hymn is an effective way to improve congregational singing.

a. *Bold intonations.* With a familiar hymn, use a brief intonation as an introduction. There are several fine published collections, but it is also great fun to work out one's own.

b. *Antiphonal stanzas.* Plan simple arrangements of longer

hymns in which the congregation sits out a stanza which receives special musical treatment by the choir and/or instruments. Print clear instructions in the church bulletin.

c. *Additional instruments.* To the usual organ accompaniment, add piano, electric guitar, percussion, hand bells. Occasionally, replace the organ completely with a brass choir, jazz or rock combo, or percussion ensemble.

d. *Descant and faux-bourdon.* Descants are not usually helpful to congregational singing, as the people are somewhat bemused by the vocal pyrotechnics. Use descants only with continued strong leadership by a majority of the choir. Descants are also effective on stanzas for choir alone. A moving or running bass is not as distracting as a descant, and is often very effective in adding punch to a stirring hymn stanza.

e. *Free harmonizations* of hymn-tunes must be used with great discretion. If the new harmonization does not encourage or inspire greater congregational effort, it may be considered a failure.

f. *Pitch modulation.* A brief modulation between stanzas, with a fresh start in a new key, can give the congregation a "second wind" in a long hymn. The pitch should never be changed by more than a half-step up or down.

Introducing Unfamiliar Hymns

Fuss and fanfare about introducing a new hymn is neither necessary nor desirable. Churchgoers have a generally conservative attitude about hymns: they like what they know. Much ado about "Now we are going to sing a new hymn" may escalate latent suspicion into open antagonism.

a. Introduce unfamiliar hymns regularly, but not frequently. One new hymn a month will keep the congregation's repertory growing steadily, but won't provoke overt resistance.

b. Be certain that the proposed new hymn is worth adding to the congregational repertory. Hymnals abound in those that aren't.

c. New hymns must win their own way, they cannot be "sold" to the congregation. If a new tune is genuinely attractive, people will want to sing it, and can do so with little difficulty. The best hymn-tunes have a folk-song character; an average person can learn them readily by rote.

d. Test new or unfamiliar hymns on the choir. If the choristers like them, so will the congregation. But if the choir has difficulty with a new tune, don't inflict it on the congregation.

e. Choir, pastor, and organist should lead the congregation in the singing of a new hymn with obvious confidence and unfeigned enjoyment. The organist should introduce the new tune with the melody on a strong solo stop. The choir should sing all stanzas in unison.

f. A hymn worth learning is worth scheduling regularly in the worship services. Any hymn that is sung once in two or three years will remain an unfamiliar hymn almost indefinitely.

Looseleaf Hymn-Sheets; The Seed of Revolution

A denominational hymnal is generally the product of a monopoly, produced as it is by the official church publishing house. In the past, the local parish church has had little choice except to purchase and use this one book. Practically speaking, the only hymns and responses available to the congregation were those included in the officially sanctioned hymnal.

This monopolistic system has had a stultifying effect on the production of new congregational music. Denominational hymnals are typically revised about once in a generation, every 25 to 35 years. Since the chances of a new or original piece of music being included in such a hymnal are almost nil, there has been no real incentive for composers to try to create new hymns or liturgical responses.

By way of contrast, in the time when almost no new hymns have been produced, tens of thousands of new choir anthems have been written. While a new hymn can find neither a publisher nor a market, choir music can. Publishing choral octavos is a highly competitive, free-enterprise business; almost any worthwhile choral music has a good chance of being published and offered for the use of churches of all denominations.

It is possible that the advent of looseleaf hymn-sheets will put this highly productive, free-enterprise system to work in the field of congregational music as well. With several or many publishers printing hymns in looseleaf form, the parish church can assemble a hymn collection of its very own, selecting the most suitable hymns not from a single source but from many.[1]

With the looseleaf concept, a new hymn need not await the publication of a new hymnal but could be printed on a single sheet

---

[1]Among publishers offering looseleaf hymns: GIA Publications, 2115 W 63rd St., Chicago, Ill. 60636. F.E.L. Publications, Ltd., 1307 So. Wabash Ave., Chicago, Ill. 60605. Vanguard Music Corp., 250 W 57th St., New York, N.Y.

and sold at modest cost in quantity. As with choral music, this new congregational music could be offered to an ecumenical market, not a denominational one. The possibility of immediate publication and wide sale of congregational hymns could greatly stimulate the creative efforts of many gifted composers who currently write only choir music.

The looseleaf concept also allows the local congregation to select and purchase exactly the hymns and responses which it intends to use. Presently, a typical denominational hymnal contains about 600 hymns. It is estimated that the typical congregation, however, uses from 50 to 100 of these. Obviously, local churches have been buying and paying for a great deal of material which they neither need nor use—a hidden cost of monopoly.

With looseleaf hymns, new congregational music can be added at any time. Equally important, materials which have outlived their usefulness can be set aside.

EXPLORING THE SOUND OF ECUMENICAL CHRISTIAN WORSHIP

Dramatizing Liturgy and Ritual

No change in the worship ritual can be made without the permission of the pastor. But if he is agreeable, there are exciting possibilities for the choir to break out of the routine of responses, anthems, and motets, and to include in the church service some unusual music.

a. *Change the liturgical music.* Occasionally, in place of the ritual music found in the hymnal or service book, use an entirely different musical setting for the liturgy. An astonishing variety of musical styles is available:

- Ancient Unison Chant: Coptic, Byzantine, Gregorian.
- Polyphonic: Palestrina, Vittoria, Lotti, etc.
- Baroque: Haydn, Handel, Bach, etc.
- Classical: Mozart, Beethoven, Schubert.
- Romantic: Gounod, Franck, Brahms, Mendelssohn.
- Contemporary: Willan, Poulenc, Peloquin, Gretchaninov, Roff, Stravinsky.
- Popular: Jazz, Folk, Rock.
- Exotic: Spanish, Latin American, Asian, African.

In using these distinctive musical settings, preserve the flavor by using the instrumentation which the composer specifies, whether string ensemble, Congo drums, brass choir, or jazz combo.

b. Where it is not practical to perform an entire mass (and this may be in most churches), use only one or two portions. In this way, the congregation's role is not unduly unsurped by the choir. Where a hymnbook, "Holy, Holy, Holy," is used in the service, substitute the Sanctus from Schubert's "Mass in G," or from the African "Missa Luba" (Lawson-Gould 51504). Instead of reciting the creed every Sunday, occasionally use a dramatic musical setting such as the Credo from Gounod's "Messe Solennelle" (St. Cecelia), or perhaps the deeply devout "Credo" of A. Gretchaninov (Boston Music Co. #1068).

c. *Singing the service propers.* Introits, graduals, and collect prayers may be sung instead of being recited. There are whole collections of great "Amens" and "Alleluias" which can be used in the service in place of the simple and utilitarian settings normally found in the hymnals.

d. *Singing the scripture lessons.* Many anthems and motets are actually portions of scripture which can be presented in a forceful and memorable way. Assume that the gospel to be read is Matthew 21:1-9. The minister should begin the reading quite as usual... "And the crowds that went before him and that followed him shouted...," and at that instant the choir should break in with a choral setting which is the continuation of this gospel: "Hosanna to the Son of David! Blessed is he who comes in the name of the Lord! Hosanna in the highest!"[2]

There are dozens of great anthem and motet texts which are suitable for imaginative and dramatic use in the church service.

Chanting the Psalms and Canticles

Most choirs and congregations experience considerable difficulty in learning new chants. The problem stems from a radical difference between chants and the usual run of music. Biblical psalms and canticles are prose; they have neither the rhyme nor meter which are so characteristic of Western poetry.

Before the Reformation, texts were always in Latin, and special tunes were created for each of the commonly used prose texts; this

----

[2] A very practical version of this particular gospel passage can be found in Buszin: *Praetorius Settings for A Cappella Choir.* Schmidt, Hall, and McCreary; Auditorium Series #19.

was plainsong. During the Reformation, the psalms and canticles were translated from Latin into the vernaculars, often cast into rhymed and metered poetry as well, as typified by the Ainsworth and Genevan Psalters, or the psalm paraphrases of Isaac Watts. In rhymed and metrical versions, the psalms could readily be sung to familiar and popular tunes of that day.

Not all translations were in rhyme and meter; many were vernacular prose. For these, it was necessary to devise new non-metrical melodies. Melodies created for the singing of religious prose are called chants.

Three Systems of Chant: Plainsong, Anglican, Gelineau

In chant, it is basic that the text governs the tune. Musical phrases are extended or contracted to fit the length of each successive phrase of the text. The rhythm of the speech controls the rhythm in the melody.

Plainsong was developed in the Medieval church; it is pure melody. Through centuries of use, the psalm tunes became exquisitely adapted to the Latin versions of the psalms and canticles. Some feel that plainsong does not adapt as successfully to languages other than Latin. Plainsong should be sung unison or antiphonally, preferably a cappella.

Anglican chant was developed in England following the "Act of Uniformity" of 1549. This Act made mandatory the use of the English-language *Book of Common Prayer* in all of the churches of the land. Latin, and the psalm tunes used with Latin were suppressed. In conformity with the Act, the psalms were translated into English prose, and a new system of semi-metrical, homophonically harmonized chant was devised. In this Anglican system of chant, the closing syllables of each phrase are sung metrically, while the duration of the reciting tone is adjusted to the length of the prose-phrase.

Anglican chants may be sung in unison or parts, and typically are accompanied by the organist. A feature of Anglican chant is that tunes are to a large degree interchangeable. Almost any psalm can be "pointed" (arranged) to be sung with almost any chant tune. While this has a certain utilitarian advantage, it has resulted in the development of bland, commonplace tunes, quite devoid of musical character. In Anglican chant, any close relationship between text and tune is accidental.

Gelineau psalmody is a modern system of chant which first

attracted wide attention in the 1950's. The chants, devised by Fr. Joseph Gelineau, a French Jesuit, are based upon equal measures of whole notes, which are subdivided as required by the word rhythm. Gelineau tunes are not interchangeable; each is designed to fit a specific psalm or canticle. The tunes may be sung in unison or in parts. Many have been arranged for accompaniment by various combinations of instruments.

Save Time with Note-for-Word Transcriptions

In most church choirs, the only chants that are well sung are those which have been memorized. This is no problem with chants that are frequently used, but memorization takes an inordinate amount of rehearsal time when chants are used only on rare occasions.

As an alternative to memorization, transcribe the occasional chant from its conventional (and confusing) format into a lucid note-for-word version. In this form, almost any choir can quickly master any chant, in any style, at a great saving of rehearsal time. (See Illustration 6-2.)

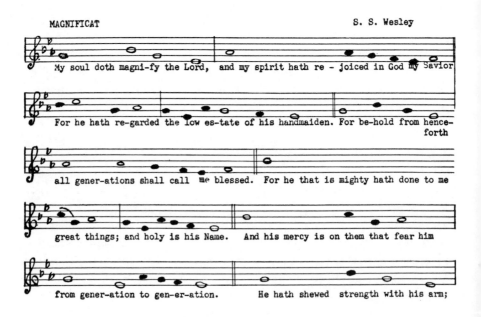

Illustration 6-2

7 Interpreting Choral Scores

TO TEACH, LEARN; TO LEAD, STUDY

The "Secret of Success" Is the Study of Scores

Arturo Toscanini was once asked what he considered to be the secret of his remarkable success as a conductor. He replied simply, "All my life I have been studying scores."

The most basic knowledge that is required of a conductor, whether amateur or professional, is the total, comprehensive mastery of his score. Lacking this, a conductor is merely bluffing, as the musicians in his care will quickly discover.

A church choir is usually just as good as its director; never better, seldom worse. A choir, as Leland Sateren observes, can learn anything you can teach it. Thus, improvement in the choir is inevitably contingent upon an improvement in the ability of its leadership.

Only Superior Knowledge Sustains the Director's Authority

To be effective, a conductor must have "authority." Unfortunately, "authority" cannot be obtained on demand; it must be earned from one's fellow-musicians. Performers respect only one kind of conductor: the one who knows more about the music than they do.

A sometimes conspicuous weakness among church choir directors is a lack of intimate and detailed knowledge of anthem scores. A generalized knowledge of music is not sufficient, although many seem tempted to try to get along with this. Only the director who knows every note and word in every voice line is an absolutely reliable guide and leader in the exploration of music. Such knowledge is attained through diligent score study, and in no other way.

Authority Is Undermined by Ignorance or Carelessness

A choral score contains two kinds of material: matters of fact and matters of opinion. You must be 100% certain concerning matters of fact. In matters of taste and opinion, you must develop a sensible position, tenable under attack, if it comes to that.

But knowing what is correct is not sufficient. The director must insist that the music be correctly performed by his singers, which is quite another matter. As rehearsals progress, every detail of the score should be scrupulously enforced by the director. If he permits mezzo-forte singing in a passage clearly marked pianissimo, the singers must conclude that their director either has overlooked the marking or does not care whether they sing correctly or not. Either conclusion is certain to diminish their respect for the musical ability and authority of their director.

Solve Your Problems at Home, the Choir's at Rehearsal

The experienced director has observed that the better he knows the music, the faster his singers will learn it. Conversely, the ill-prepared director is an obstacle in the path of learning for his choir. It just isn't possible to be an effective teacher if one is "learning the music along with the choir." The bluffer is betrayed by dozens of little errors, and choristers have an uncanny knack for seeing through his attempts to cover these with bluster.

The director, in his role as leader, sets goals, determines the line of travel, and controls the rate of progress. Your choir can go just about as far and as fast as you yourself are willing to travel. Your enthusiasm for music, your loyalty to the church and its ideals will be reflected by your singers. The church choir director who is not prepared to give his very best to the job can scarcely expect his singers to do so.

Conducting is a lifelong study. As Claudio Abbado remarked, "There is never a moment when one has arrived. You have to study all your life!" There are no more "born" conductors than there are "born" violinists; such skills must be learned. And like other musical skills, choral conducting requires regular and consistent practice and study. As a lifelong student of his art, the church choirmaster must expect to study and practice 30 to 60 minutes, *each and every day.*

A choral score ought to be studied until you can "hear a perfect performance in your head." Know precisely how the music should sound before your choristers ever see an anthem for a first reading.

EQUIPPING FOR IN-DEPTH SCORE STUDY

The church choir director can study scores more efficiently if he has the necessary equipment.

a. *Keyboard instrument.* A piano or home organ is a practical instrument for gaining a first impression of a new choral score. However, it must be remembered that the instrument does not sound at all like a voice. Music sung will sound very different from the same music played.

b. *Metronome.* This device is absolutely essential to confirm indicated tempos.

c. *Music dictionary.* This reference source is useful in checking the meaning of unfamiliar terms and markings in the score.

d. *Music encyclopedia.* A large and comprehensive reference work such as *Grove's* is invaluable. Much information on composers, musical mechanics, and music history can be obtained from this one source.

e. *The Bible* (in several translations, traditional and contemporary). This is, after all, *the* sourcebook for nearly all religious music in the Western world.

f. *Concordance to the Bible.* This index to the Bible is quite indispensable in tracking down the Scriptural source of anthem texts which are only vaguely identified in the octavo.

g. *Bible commentaries.* These can often make clear, perhaps vivid, the meaning of obscure or difficult words and phrases in anthem texts.

h. *Hymnals of several kinds.* Hymn stanzas comprise the text of many anthems. It is often helpful, and always interesting, to read the hymn in its original version.

i. *Hymnal commentary and indices.* Many denominations publish a hymnal companion or commentary, giving the background about hymns, their authors or sources, and their composers. The circumstances in which a hymn was created often make a fascinating story which further illumines the meaning of the hymn.

FIRST STEPS IN SCORE STUDY

Researching the Background

A good first step in score study is research on the composer and the author or source of his text:

- When did they live?
- Where did they work?
- How were music and text brought together?
- Why was this piece written?
- Is this an excerpt from a larger work?
- What was the original form of this music? To what extent has it been edited, altered, or transcribed?

Record significant information on the Performance Register. If this octavo-size memo is always kept with the director's copy of each anthem, the information will be readily available to share with the choir during rehearsal.

Knowledge of the background of music helps to mark the director as a well-informed specialist in his chosen field.

Identify the Fundamental Structure of the Music

A second step in score study is the identification of its basic form or musical structure:

- Is it prose or poetry?
- Does it have regular meter and stanzas?
- Does the text repeat with variations in the musical setting?
- Is there a regular refrain or chorus?

In some music, each measure is unique and never repeated. In others, there may be only 12 or 16 bars of music, which may be repeated three or four times with different words.

Discover the Emotional Key

As a third step, define in one or two words the prevailing emotional tone of each section of the anthem. Perhaps the emotional tone remains constant from beginning to end, but often there is a marked change in mood within an anthem. The correct identification of emotional tone is of vital importance in the subsequent study and performance of the work.

UNDERSTANDING THE TEXT

In Choral Music, Text Determines All

Choral music is, in essence, program music. The text provides the "program"; it is the key to a correct interpretation of the music. Musical techniques are used by the composer to illumine the meaning of the text. Skill in choral writing can rightly be understood and appreciated only in its relation to the text. Not all competent composers are good at choral writing, and some great composers have left us some very awkward pages of music for chorus.

Read It Before You Sing It

Expressive choral singing originates in expressive language. Speak the text, using the tempo, dynamics, and accents indicated in the score. In well-written choral music, the expression markings fit just as well with oral reading as with singing. In a convincing performance of choral music, the musical expression grows out of the text in a natural and logical manner. Dynamics, especially, should never call attention to themselves, nor impress one as "tacked on" accessories.

Research Unfamiliar Words and Phrases

Look up the correct pronunciation and meaning of any unfamiliar word which appears in the text. Being certain of such details is part of the expertise expected of a first-rank choral director.

What is the "Balm in Gilead" mentioned in the famous spiritual?

What is the "Wail of Euroclydon" in Neale's hymn, "Fierce was the wild billow"?

At times, the director must select between alternate pronunciations (either, amen). Use the pronunciation which is current in your locality.

Foreign Languages. To sing in a language other than English is seldom required of an American church choir. Singing worship music in Latin or German because this was the original tongue makes as little sense in church as for the liturgist to read the gospel in the original Greek. If the congregation cannot understand, why bother?

There are, of course, some classic works in Latin which have thus far defied effective adaptation to English texts. Here we must use the original or not sing them at all. But the frequent use of such works in the worship service cannot be justified.

In singing Latin, it is well to remember that there is no universally accepted "correct" pronunciation of Latin. Many American Catholic clergy speak Latin in an Italianate manner,[1] as they were trained in Rome. But choirs in France or Germany sing Latin

---

[1] A pamphlet, "Pronunciation of Church Latin," expounds the Italian system. Available from the American Guild of Organists, 630 Fifth Ave., New York, N.Y. 10020.

quite differently from the Italians, as a comparison of phonograph recordings will clearly reveal.

Seek Spiritual Insight

Mastery of correct pronunciation and phonetics is of course important in choral singing. But even more important is an understanding of the spiritual thought and religious faith which undergirds the words. Singing, devoid of understanding and emotion, is merely vocal exercise. It is the message that motivates the sensitive singer. It is part of the conductor's function to sensitize his singers so that they can experience and express the spiritual values and emotions of the music.

Dull music is dull precisely because it lacks emotion. The inspired (spirit-filled) singer expresses emotion in many small but natural ways: his posture, general demeanor, style of diction, quality of tone, control of dynamics.

In some types of choral music, emotions are on the surface and obvious. In other kinds, emotions are subtle, transitory, and evanescent. These latter require careful analysis and deep insight. As an exercise, define the emotions of Jesus and Mary as portrayed by Heinrich Schuetz in his dialogue for Easter, "Woman, Why Weepest Thou?" (Concordia 97-6369).

The impact of choral music lies not in the correct production of mere syllables and notes, however important this may be, but in the spiritual ideas and emotions which underlie these. To miss these is to miss the whole reason for singing.

ANALYZING THE COMPOSER'S RESPONSE TO THE TEXT

Why Did He Write It This Way?

The form of the music, its rhythm, melodies, harmonies, and dynamics, result from the composer's response to his text. To understand choral music, the director-student should ask at every phrase:

- What does the composer want here?
- Why did he write it this way?

Each Composer Responds in His Own Way

Composers are intensely individual; each responds to words and ideas in his own personal way. Each uses his own musical language to express that response. Even when composers use exactly the same text, such as the liturgical "Kyrie" or "Sanctus," their response to that text, and their musical exposition of it is unique and individual. Bruckner's musical language is not like Bach's, nor is Bach's like Vittoria's or Mozart's. Each in his own time and place has tried to illumine the meaning of his text, using the most expressive musical techniques at his command.

In well-written choral music, there is a reason for everything that appears in the score. It is the director's mission to discover that reason.

Finding the Key Words and Phrases

In each phrase or sentence, some words are more important than others. What has the composer done to emphasize these? Look for these musical devices:

- Key words have a prominent position in the melodic line.
- They are held longer for emphasis.
- They may be louder or softer than adjacent words.
- They may be strongly accented.
- They may be strikingly harmonized to set them apart. (Example: Charles Ives' 22-note tone cluster on the word "wrath" in "Psalm 90.")
- Voicing changes may be emphatic, viz. from parts to unison or unison to parts in a key phrase.

Evaluating Interpretative Markings

A clear distinction should be made between markings placed in the score by composers themselves and those which have been added by others. Prior to the 18th century, composers seldom included interpretative markings in their manuscripts. About the time of Bach and Handel, composers began to write in a very few indications of speed and loudness.

Most published editions of early choral music now include interpretative markings. These reflect the opinions of editors or arrangers, who, while well-informed, are surely not infallible. There is no reason to believe, for example, that Palestrina meant his music to be performed in the way suggested in the editions of J. Varley Roberts. Such editorial markings are not sacrosanct, and if they don't work out in performance, the director has every right to try something that will.

Interpretative suggestions made by composers should be treated with greatest deference. Contemporary composers often indicate in precise detail how a work is to be performed. Until proven definitely incorrect or ineffective, composers' markings should be considered inviolable.

Determining Tempo

Perhaps no feature of music is as subject to arbitrary opinion and capricious change as tempo. Artists of first rank play the same piece at entirely different speeds. Symphonic conductors late in their careers may use tempi entirely different from those which they earlier considered correct. A radical change in tempo can alter the whole character of the music; "Yankee Doodle" played slowly enough could pass for a church hymn. A correct tempo is absolutely essential to a satisfactory musical performance. But what is a correct tempo?

When the score carries a generalized indication of tempo, such as *andante,* check your metronome. The range of *andante* is often considered MM 126-152. Try the piece at each of these extremes, then settle for the precise MM speed which seems appropriate to the text and comfortable for the choir.

In ornate or highly embellished music, any tempo that obscures note patterns or obliterates the text is too fast for effective performance. Choral music must have time to "sound" (reverberate) in its environment. A large choir in a large auditorium must sing more slowly than a small choir in an intimate chapel, to allow for the longer reverberation time in the larger hall.

The first practical metronome appeared in 1816 during Beethoven's time. Metronome indications in editions of music composed prior to this time are not authentic. They may be useful guides, but if they don't work out in performance, one should not feel guilty about changing them.

Bar-Lines and Micro-Rhythms

Rhythm is the great organizing force in music. Rhythm is the heartbeat of music, and if it ebbs or fails, music dies.

Rhythm should not be confused with meter. In song, true rhythm is found in the words, not in the repetitious meter of a tune.

Bar-Lines. Composers did not use measures (bar-lines) until the end of the 16th century. It is said that Palestrina had seen bar-lines in the works of others but did not choose to use them in his own manuscripts. Bar-lines appearing in the published editions of Palestrina have been added by editors.

It must be admitted that bar-lines are a great convenience to conductors and singers in the study and rehearsal of music. But in the performance of choral music, these measure-markers should be ignored. All attention ought to focus on the phrase, not the measure. In march music or dance music, a slight accent on the downbeat is typical and appropriate. But such accents in religious choral music destroy the shape of the phrase; rhythm is thus sacrificed to meter.

Count the Micro-Rhythms. It is not enough for a conductor to think in quarter-notes; his subconscious metronome should pulse in sixteenth-notes (four to each beat). Only in this way can note values, especially combinations of dotted notes, be measured with accuracy.

Melody, Harmony, and the Relation of Voice-Lines

Melody. Identify the mode or scale upon which each melody is constructed. Many of the greatest early chorales were derived from Medieval church modes, and still retain something of this character. Many folk-songs and spirituals are built on the pentatonic scale (can be played on the five black notes on the keyboard). Being able to identify melodic features is part of professional expertise.

Harmony. This is a combination of melodies. In homophonic writing, the great problem is the monotony (sometimes literal monotony) of the melodies in the inner or lower voices. It's very hard to keep the altos enthusiastic about a voice-part that drones along on a span of three to four notes. In general, such impoverished choral writing should be eliminated from the repertory.

Relation of Voice-Lines. Effective voice-pairings mark good choral composition. The alert singer, like the experienced square-dancer, should be aware of a change of partners and alter his singing style to suit that of his companions. Tenors, for example, may sing less robustly in a S-A-T combination than in a T-B-B voicing. The director should note all such combinations and prepare to assist his singers in these adjustments.

Note also canons and other contrapuntal devices. Demonstrate these to the choir at the first reading of the anthem.

Try to understand the composer's reasons for every change of key or voicing, his use of striking harmonies, dynamic changes, or rhythmic patterns. If the music is well constructed, these features are always closely related to episodes in the text.

Dynamics: Energy Employed Expressively

Circle with colored pencil every dynamic marking in the score. In song, as in expressive speech, changes in dynamics should appear to grow out of the ideas in the text, and not seem superimposed.

Church choral music is not by nature loud music. The whole scale of dynamics should be modest rather than bombastic. It is best to err on the quiet side.

Pauses: Breathing, Punctuation, Phrasing

Singers must breathe. Left on their own, amateurs like to take a nip of breath about every two measures, whether this makes musical sense or not. During score study, mark the breathing places that are both practical and logical.

Expressing Punctuation. In writing or speaking, punctuation is an important aid in clarifying communication. The expression of punctuation is equally important in singing, and for the same purpose. A skilled oral reader interprets commas, or semicolons, or periods with voice inflections and subtle pauses. A text-conscious choir should do exactly the same.

In singing, commas are likely to be the most troublesome and controversial of punctuation markings. Should the choir express every comma with a pause? Or should the singers plow right over the commas as if they didn't exist? Should some commas be expressed and others ignored? Decide these things as you study and mark your score accordingly.

Delineating the Phrase. In song, each phrase is part of a continuing story. A phrase ending is not a terminus; each should lift into the next, so that the piece is a whole, not disjointed with many little stops and starts.

This does not mean that phrases should be run together, even for the sake of a "long line" of music. In choral singing, the cardinal principle is clarity of communication. Phrasings should be edited (or re-edited) for the greatest possible ease of understanding.

Fermatas in Chorales. Ordinarily a fermata indicates a "hold." This is not always the case with fermatas in chorales. In a chorale, the fermata is usually a relic of an extinct 18th century custom, whereby the organist embellished his playing of the hymn with cadenzas or brief free improvisations, much like a "break" or "lick" in jazz. Fermatas in chorales simply indicate phrase endings where such optional ornamentation might be inserted. To interpret all these fermatas as holds can result in a grotesque distortion of both the melody and the text. If it makes no sense to interpret them as holds, fermatas should be marked out of the music.

Rationalizing Choral Accompaniments

Except in a cappella performances, the formulation of an effective, yet practical instrumental accompaniment is a vital part of score study. At the very least, this would include a carefully rationalized organ registration. As often as practical, it should include provision for the use of auxiliary instruments. Sometimes such instruments are suggested in the keyboard accompaniment, such as the oboe so effectively used in Hovhaness' "Watchman, Tell Us of the Night" (C. F. Peters, #6460).

Increasingly, contemporary composers and arrangers of church music are scoring for modest instrumental combinations. But the older favorites in the choral library can be given a fresh sound with an imaginative re-voicing of the organ part, or, in some cases, through the restoration of an original instrumentation. How about a small orchestra on that chorus lifted from a Bach cantata? Why not try "Silent Night, Holy Night" with the original guitar accompaniment?

ADAPTING MUSIC FOR LOCAL PERFORMANCE

Exercising Musical Imagination

Relatively little music is performed in precisely the manner envisioned by the composer. Changing conditions of performance have made adaptations, arrangements, editions, and translations a major part of the music business. Much of the success of the church music director will depend upon his musical imagination; his ability to adapt published versions to his own circumstances and musical resources. Musical *knowledge* is important; it tells the director how the work ought to be performed. But musical *imagination* is priceless; it suggests how the music may actually be performed *in your church,* with your resources and physical facilities.

Adapting music for local conditions is certainly nothing new. Michael Praetorius in the early 1600's created a whole series of chorale arrangements for performance by multiple choirs, or choir and congregation, with or without organ or other instruments. Their flexibility was limited only by the musical imagination of the director.[2]

---

[2]See especially: "All Glory Be to God on High," ed. Carl Schalk, Augsburg, 11-1609; "Christ Our Lord, Who Died to Save Us," ed. Carl Schalk, Augsburg, ACL 11-1608.

Eliminating Unnecessary Difficulties

Choral music is not always thoroughly tested in performance prior to publication. Some capable and prolific anthem composers do not currently direct church choirs. These may tend to write for an idealized choir, in which human frailty and fallibility are not factors. Church anthems as published rather frequently contain booby-traps, visual hazards, and plain errors. In score study, be alert for such, and attempt to avoid all such perils.

Booby-Traps. The classic booby-trap in the church anthem is the extended a cappella passage, followed by an entrance for organ. If the choir strays slightly from absolute pitch (as some have been known to do), the organ chord instantly advertises this error to all. Avoid this booby-trap by using light organ support throughout for a "quasi-a cappella effect" that will keep the choir on pitch.

Visual Hazards. These are certain things in a score which the singers may overlook or misinterpret: important instructions in small print; a sudden entrance at a page-turn; a voice-part that appears in an unexpected place on the great staff; unobtrusively printed changes of key or meter. Mark every such hazard in colored pencil.

Music manuscript is to most amateur choristers a visual hazard. Accustomed to neatly printed, carefully aligned notes and words, singers are often upset by the vagaries of handwork. Generally, it will take longer for a choir to learn music from manuscript than from printed copies.

Errors. In score study, correct all typographical errors. An apparent error in the voice-line can often be confirmed by referring to the accompaniment or keyboard reduction; rarely will both be found in error. Errors should be corrected in the choir copies by the librarians before the music is distributed to the singers.

Adding Your Own Interpretative Markings

Interpretative markings are just as much a part of the music as are notes and words. Choristers should be taught to observe and obey whatever marks appear in the score; compliance should not be left to individual whim. Musical discipline is badly undermined if the director permits his singers to ignore musical markings in rehearsal, or, even worse, instructs them deliberately to disobey these. If the director prefers an interpretation of the music different from the printed edition, he should have his changes pencilled into the singers' copies.

Comprehensive Interpretative Cues. It is often helpful if additional performance instructions are pencilled into the choristers' copies. These may include indications for the more precise timing of consonants, the exact sound of a vowel, comprehensive marks for articulation or accentuation of notes, places to breathe, treatment of punctuation, and the like.

If the librarians will do this prior to rehearsal, much time can be saved. If the changes are to be dictated to the choir in rehearsal, have the singers first number each measure in the piece. Then, measure by measure, or note by note, marks may be added. This is quite time consuming and subject to considerable error. It is far preferable if the changes are made by the librarians.

SCORE SYNTHESIS: MENTALIZING A PERFECT PERFORMANCE

Hearing Music in the Mind's Ear

The final step in score study is synthesis—fitting all the details and little pieces together like parts of a puzzle. In this process, the director mentalizes a perfect total performance of the music—before his singers see the first page of the music.

This "performance in the head" should be comprehensive. Know exactly how you want every phrase of the music to sound. In the mind's-ear, hear the attacks in perfect intonation, a beautiful choral tone, crisp diction with perfectly timed consonants. In a fully developed synthesis, you can almost sense the emotional vibrations emanating from your imaginary choir.

Respecting the Composer's Intentions

The conductor's first responsibility is not to himself, but to the music. Music is not merely a vehicle for expressing the performer's personality; rather, the performer is a vehicle for the expression of the music. As Lorin Maazel points out: "The only thing that counts in musicianship is passionate love for what the composer has written down, and the knowledge of how best to interpret it."[3]

Seldom is there only one "right" way to interpret a musical score. The most capable and perceptive artists may at times differ greatly. Dr. Albert Schweitzer played Bach's chorale preludes much more slowly than other great interpreters. But was he wrong and they

[3]Interview in *Life* magazine, Feb 21, 1969, p. 49.

right? Talented actors do not read Hamlet's soliloquy in a precisely identical manner. Each repeats the same words but inflects and interprets them in an individual style. Yet all share a common goal: conveying as clearly as possible the inmost thoughts of the Danish Prince.

It is so with choral interpreters (conductors). Each has access to the same notes and words in the score. But each chooses certain features to be emphasized, in an effort to reveal the inner meaning of the music in the most lucid manner.

The conductor ought to feel a genuine respect for every bit of music which he conducts. And for the greatest music, he may indeed feel the "passionate love" of which Mr. Maazel speaks. Lacking this respect and love for the music we perform, we may in fact become, as St. Paul suggests, no more than "noisy gongs and clanging cymbals."

Becoming a Master-Musician, One Anthem at a Time

A conductor is essentially a teacher. The true maestro is, in fact, a master-teacher with a complete knowledge of the music which he will conduct. Through intensive score study (analysis and synthesis), the church choir director can, in his limited field, become a master-teacher, one anthem at a time. You need not know everything about the whole field of music but you should certainly be a leading authority on next Sunday's anthem.

Memorization of the score is a great advantage to the director in rehearsal. With the score in your head instead of your head in the score, you can concentrate your full attention on the problems of the singers. You can move away from the podium, giving special assistance when and where it is needed. Most important, you can establish eye contact with the singers, communicating through small gestures and facial expressions, which are perhaps the most effective means at your disposal.

8 Planning and Conducting Effective Rehearsals

GOOD REHEARSALS ASSURE GOOD PERFORMANCE

Rehearsals Make or Break the Choir

Rehearsals are a pivotal factor in the success of the church music program. For it is here that the real work of the choir is done . . . or not done.

Music can fulfill its spiritual mission only after the singers have gained a reasonable mastery of the mechanics of performance. Music poorly prepared in rehearsal will be poorly sung in performance, and will be of slight benefit, spiritual or aesthetic, to the congregation, choir, clergy, or conductor.

Careful Planning Conserves Rehearsal Time

A typical church choir rehearses for about 90 minutes, once each week. With rehearsal time so severely limited, it is mandatory that the director plan his rehearsal so carefully that each of these minutes will be profitably invested. He must employ rehearsal methods and teaching techniques that will insure a rapid rate of learning with a high degree of retention. The successful choral conductor is a superb teacher—skilled, organized, and highly motivated.

Make Each Rehearsal a Stimulating Musical Adventure

The verb "to rehearse" comes from an old French agricultural term, meaning "to rake over" or "to harrow"—breaking down the clods and lumps to the desired fineness.

Too often, rehearsing is equated to laborious drudgery, the price that singers must pay for the privilege of performing music in public. Quite to the contrary, the church choir rehearsal should be in itself an exciting and stimulating musical adventure. For each meeting with the choir, the leader should prepare activities designed not only to teach the singer how to perform the music well, but which will increase his understanding of the music and his appreciation of its message.

In conducting the rehearsal, the director should radiate genuine enthusiasm for the music; if he can't honestly do this, he has scheduled the wrong music. His attitude in rehearsal should be unfailingly cheerful, optimistic, and encouraging. For choristers, each rehearsal should be a joyous occasion, a high point of the week. A musical evening (rehearsal) must not be wasted on dull anthems or boring drillwork; nor should singers be expected to accept abuse from an ill-tempered tyrant of a director.

Plan each rehearsal so that at its conclusion, the singer will feel that—

- His time has been well spent.
- He would have missed much by not attending.
- He has read some interesting music.
- He can sing better than ever before.
- He has encountered significant spiritual ideas.
- He has learned at least one thing he didn't know before.

EFFECTIVE REHEARSALS REQUIRE THOROUGH PLANNING

Prepare a Comprehensive Written Outline

The director must control his rehearsal. A comprehensive written outline of rehearsal activities will give him a secure track to run on. A rehearsal plan might include:

- Time to rehearse all music for six to seven weeks ahead.
- A vocal exercise.
- An experiment in seating.
- Biographical notes on composer or author.
- A "chalk talk" of two to three minutes.
- Illustrative excerpt from a phonograph recording.
- Pictures, charts, or diagrams relevant to the music.
- An analysis of the musical structure of one piece.

Planned Progress Eliminates "Cramming"

Choirs learn more efficiently through spaced learning than they do by cramming. In learning a motet, 15 minutes at each of six successive rehearsals will accomplish more than 90 minutes in one big dose. Superior choir performance results from preparation that moves forward each week on a regular and controlled schedule.

The rehearsal plan will thus include music in various stages of preparation. Some will be read for the first time. Several may just be roughed-in, merely beginning to take shape. Others will be receiving their final polish prior to performance.

Test Every Detail in Rehearsal; Leave Nothing to Chance

The rehearsal plan should include a review of the service music: hymns, psalms, responses, chants, liturgy, as well as anthems and motets. Such review should eliminate awkward uncertainty in the worship service.

Positioning the Instruments. If instruments other than organ are to be used with the choir, these should be rehearsed under actual performance conditions, and not just in the rehearsal room. Brass, percussion, and electronic instruments can generate enormous tonal energy in comparison with voices; they must be very carefully positioned in the church—tonally balanced to the total ensemble.

Testing the Seating Plan. If any deviation from normal choir seating is planned, allow time in the rehearsal plan to test the new arrangement. If, for example, you plan an echo choir singing from a balcony, be certain that the idea is thoroughly tested in the rehearsal.

Checking Organ Registration. As often as practical, part of each rehearsal should be conducted in the sanctuary with the organ. Director and organist will then have an opportunity to evaluate ensemble balance. The singers also can become accustomed to the organ registration, which is very different in sound from the rehearsal room piano.

Allow time in your rehearsal plan to test every detail; insofar as possible, leave nothing to chance.

Control the Pace of the Rehearsal

A choir rehearsal should start with relatively easy material; drive hardest as soon as the singers are warmed up (but still fresh), then gradually ease off with well-learned music towards the close.

Hymn-singing is an excellent opening activity. Sing hymns a cappella, in parts, as beautifully and expressively as possible. Hymns are not vocally taxing, and they help to set an appropriate spiritual tone to the rehearsal. They usually have a good choral sound, encouraging the singers to listen to each other. If they are well sung, hymns are a satisfying first experience in the rehearsal.

Liturgy or service responses may be rehearsed immediately after the hymns.

Vocal exercises or experiments should come early in the rehearsal, if they are to be used at all. Exercises should occupy no more than 3 to 5% of the rehearsal time; about three minutes in a 90-minute session.

New or difficult music should come next, occupying 40-50% of the total rehearsal time. The most difficult problems should be attacked while minds and voices are fresh and alert.

Familiar repertory, which can be sung with greater ease, should be scheduled in the latter part of the rehearsal period. End the session with the choir's very best singing. The last impression of the rehearsal, like the first, should leave the singer pleased, encouraged, and confident.

Accomplish Something with Every Anthem Scheduled

Make it an absolute rule to spend at least some time each week with every anthem on the rehearsal schedule. Rarely can one accomplish all that he should in the time allotted to each anthem, and the temptation is to rob time from future anthems to spend on present problems. If one is really pushed for time, a straight-through reading of an average anthem may take only three or four minutes. While this may be less than originally scheduled, it is vastly better than no work at all. Something done will prove more effective than nothing done.

Using the Music Schedule as a Rehearsal Plan

If you program your choir's music in units (page 120), the published schedule is virtually a ready-made rehearsal outline. Since the schedule shows when each anthem will be sung, it is very easy to compute each week the number of rehearsals remaining until performance. With this information, you can then allocate an appropriate amount of time to the preparation of each selection.

PREPARING YOURSELF FOR THE REHEARSAL

Getting Ready to Conduct the World's Finest Choir

Let's pretend:

A famous professional choir is scheduled to give a concert in your community. You have been invited to appear as guest conductor, directing Gretchaninov's "Nunc Dimittis" (Boston Music 1125). Prior to the concert, you will be allowed 20 minutes of rehearsal with the choir. How should you prepare yourself for this rehearsal and concert appearance?

Would you memorize every detail of the score?

Would you try to get "up" physically and psychologically for the brief rehearsal and the concert? Would you be especially careful to develop an artistic interpretation of the music? How would you plan to spend your precious 20 minutes of rehearsal time? Would you look forward to this event as a stimulating and exciting experience?

So much for pretending.

If you would prepare yourself carefully to direct some other choir, how carefully should you prepare yourself each week to direct your own?

It is a delusion to believe that you would work harder and become a better conductor if you were in a larger church or had a better choir. The truth is, if you work hard right where you are, you will soon become a better director and create a better choir.

Doing Your Homework

The conductor who sight-reads scores at the rehearsal is paying a supreme insult to his choir. Even the most experienced of professional conductors devote hours of study to scores which they have conducted dozens of times. The mastery of music comes only through constant study and review. *It's what you learn after you already know everything that really counts.* Review and re-study each anthem before every rehearsal. If the score is particularly difficult or quite unfamiliar, review it every day until it becomes entirely familiar.

Decide during your study periods exactly what you wish the choir to accomplish at the coming rehearsal. When your objectives are clearly defined, you have a better chance of attaining them.

Getting "Up" for Rehearsal

The choir leader who arrives at the rehearsal room physically tired, mentally weary, or emotionally upset, is not likely to be an effective conductor.

In the confines of the rehearsal room, the director's mood and attitude are highly contagious. Ill-temper, pessimism, or discouragement will quickly spread among the singers. But, fortunately, so will good-humor, patience, and confidence. For the sake of all, do not allow chance or outside circumstances to determine your rehearsal mood. Follow a regimen which will put you in the rehearsal room physically fit, mentally alert, and emotionally "up."

It is almost always helpful if you can make a complete break from your normal daily routine on rehearsal night. Take time out to relax, rest, pray, think, and reflect . . . in solitude. A shower, a cat-nap, and a change of clothing may do wonders.

Dress. Since conducting is hard physical work, comfortable, informal clothing should be appropriate. Clothes are an important form of communication, which others read with considerable accuracy. Remember, your singers want to be proud of the way you look, not feel sorry for you.

"Get Me to the Church on Time . . . " For the director, being "on time" means arriving at least 20 minutes before the start of the rehearsal. The director who rushes in breathlessly at the last minute is creating problems, not solutions. An early arrival gives you time to check everything personally, and to confer with accompanists or singers as necessary. Most important, you can then begin the rehearsal precisely at the time announced.

Emotional Pre-Conditioning

As you approach the rehearsal, your emotional condition is fully as important as your physical condition.

Gaining Emotional Control. Before leaving for the rehearsal, spend a few minutes in an emotional inventory.

a. Make certain that all personal problems are left at home, be they family, health, business, or financial. Nothing constructive can be done about such problems at the rehearsal, so don't take them along. Discipline your mind to concentrate on the music, and nothing but the music, for the duration of the rehearsal.

b. Rid yourself of emotional hangovers. It is all too easy in rehearsal to vent previously built-up anger or frustration upon the singers because they may be too polite or respectful to fight back.

c. Have absolute confidence that the rehearsal will be a stimulating and inspirational experience, because you have planned it that way. Cherish these precious minutes when you and your singers will draw away from the cares of the secular world and devote all attention to great spiritual thoughts and great musical ideas. Memorize and recite to yourself portions of the anthem texts which you and your choir will be studying. Turn your mind Godward.

d. Resolve to *encourage* your singers, no matter what happens in rehearsal. Be unfailingly constructive; correct errors without personal criticism. Continually remind yourself not to stoop to sarcasm, anger, or insulting criticism. Say nothing that could embarrass a chorister in the presence of his peers, even in jest.

e. Be confident that the singers will do their very best. Recent research indicates that school teachers who firmly believe that their pupils can and will learn are much more successful than teachers who are convinced in advance that their students are stupid, unmotivated, lazy, and incapable of learning.

Constructive Attitudes: Patience, Encouragement, Tact

All too frequently, choral conductors have an unfortunate concept of their role because they have sung or played under some trigger-tempered martinet, whom they ape, consciously or unconsciously. Professional musicians may learn to tolerate temper tantrums and torrents of verbal abuse from high-strung conductors because they get paid to do so. Singers in the volunteer church choir do not. It may be "natural" for a conductor who is deeply involved with his music to react in anger to the errors, obstructions, and frustrations of a rehearsal. But this is a "natural" reaction which we must learn to curb and divert into constructive, not destructive, channels. Anger and ill-temper, once let loose in the rehearsal room, will badly inhibit musical progress.

The attitudes which are truly helpful to the choir are not necessarily "natural" or spontaneous. Constructive attitudes need to be learned or cultivated just as much as the other skills necessary to successful conducting.

The P E T Formula. Perhaps you can recall constructive attitudes by remembering the initials P E T, standing for *P*atience, *E*ncouragement, *T*act.

Patience is the ability to endure adversity with calmness and composure. Patience is forbearance under provocation, especially the faults and limitations of others. Patience is constancy of effort.

Patience can be developed. Talk to yourself on the way to rehearsal: "Be patient . . . be patient." Believe in patience; if things go wrong in rehearsal, avoid a flash reaction. Rather, take a deep breath, remind yourself to "be patient," get control of yourself, then proceed, with infinite patience.

Encouragement is perhaps the most important thing you can give your choristers. "To encourage" means to give your courage to others, to increase their confidence, to help, to support, to inspire and stimulate by one's own example.

On the way to rehearsal, repeat F. Melius Christiansen's phrase: "Encourage . . . encourage . . . encourage . . . . . . always encourage your singers!" Make corrections in rehearsal in a way which will evoke greater effort and cooperation. Never undermine confidence nor arouse antagonism with destructive personal criticism.

Tact means "sense of touch." No one is born with tact; it is a learned ability. Tact means saying and doing the right thing. Tact is skill in dealing with people. Tact is the ability to guide others without upsetting them emotionally or physically. With tact, one handles difficult situations smoothly. Tact is saying what needs to be said without giving offense. Tact helps you to win good-will and cooperation.

Take Your P E T to Rehearsal. Before leaving for the rehearsal, the prudent director checks his briefcase to make certain that he is carrying the right scores. En route, he should also check to see that he is carrying the right attitudes. Right attitudes are just as important to the success of the rehearsal as the right music.

CHECKING REHEARSAL FACILITIES

Light, Heat, Music, Seating

As soon as you arrive at the rehearsal room, check on the readiness of the facilities.

Lights. No burnt-out lamps; no noisy, flickering fluorescent tubes.

Temperature and Ventilation. Comfortable for the singers; draft-free. No stale, musty odor.

Music Distribution. Verify proper distribution of choir copies, so that everything you intend to rehearse is in the folios. Put your own copies in the conductor's stand, arranged in the order in which you intend to call them for rehearsal.

Seating. All chairs in place, so the rehearsal need not be disrupted by revisions in the seating plan.

If you plan to hold part of the rehearsal in the chancel, a similar check of the facilities should be completed there.

Experiment with Seating Plans

There is no one right way to seat a choir. An optimum seating plan will depend on many factors: the size of the choir, the shape of the rehearsal room, the type of music to be sung. Illustration 8-1 shows several rehearsal seating plans successfully used by choral ensembles.

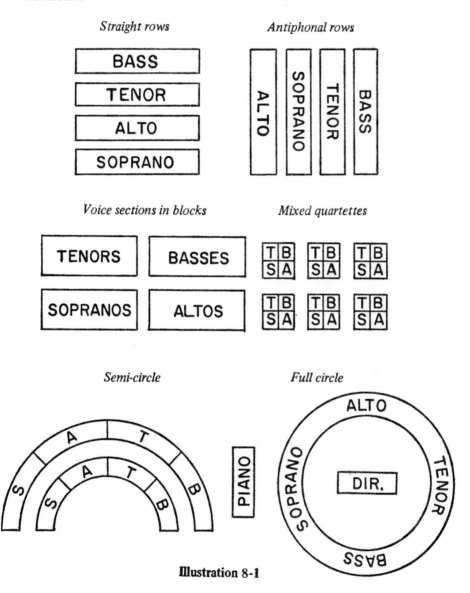

Straight rows   *Antiphonal rows*

Voice sections in blocks   *Mixed quartettes*

Semi-circle   *Full circle*

Illustration 8-1

Wherever possible, try each of these patterns; choose the most effective of the alternatives. Use a new plan for several rehearsal sessions before making a final evaluation. Encourage singers to express their opinions after adequate experience.

In any seating plan, do not allow empty seats within a section. Vacant chairs may be used to separate the voice sections, but it is best if no chairs remain unused; if there are more than one or two in a section, stop the rehearsal, have them removed, and re-seat the choir.

Preparing Visual and Audio Material

Before the rehearsal, write on the chalkboard your announcements and instructions. Post fresh materials on the bulletin board, removing outdated notices.

If you plan to tape part of the rehearsal, or demonstrate with tape or discs, set this up before the rehearsal. Precious practice time must not be frittered away on technical difficulties.

Welcome Each Singer Personally

The accompanist ought to arrive well ahead of the rehearsal hour to permit a quick conference with the director.

As the choristers begin to arrive, the director should be free to devote his entire attention to them. Try to acknowledge each with at least a smile or nod of recognition, and whenever possible, with a word of greeting or appreciation.

If the singer has a question or comment, listen most attentively. If some discussion is entailed, ask that this be postponed until after the rehearsal.

LEARNING TO LIVE WITH PROBLEMS

In Church Choirs, Difficulties Are Normal

Even if the director himself is well prepared, there remain two major causes of difficult choir rehearsals: absenteeism and a poor accompanist.

Absenteeism cannot be directly controlled by the director of a volunteer choir, although he can do much to reduce its incidence (p. 70).

A Poor accompanist is certainly no rarity, usually because he is an unprepared accompanist. One who is pre-occupied with his own problems at the keyboard cannot be very helpful to the singers. If an accompanist is chronically lax about preparing for the rehearsals, the music director must take corrective action. There is too much at stake in the rehearsal to permit sabotage by indifference or neglect.

Making Progress in Spite of Problems

No matter what difficulties arise in the rehearsal, it is imperative that the director personally show neither disappointment nor dismay. The singers are fully as conscious of problems as the director, and they will cue their reaction to his. It is useless to scold, discuss, criticize, or condemn in-absentia the missing choir members. Concentrate all attention on those who are present; ignore those who are absent.

Despite difficulties, adhere to your prepared rehearsal schedule and follow your outline. Help those who are present by working with extra energy and enthusiasm. Make certain that all who attend the rehearsal will share a real sense of satisfaction and accomplishment. Be especially alert to encourage the singers in every legitimate way; commend every good effort.

The unique talent possessed by the successful church choir director is the ability to make music sound good with whatever resources are available. Conditions in the church or choir are seldom ideal; often they are very difficult. Regard problems and frustrations as normal. The successful director is the one who has learned how to rise above adversity. "Per aspera ad astra," as the Romans used to say.

REHEARSAL TECHNIQUES THAT PRODUCE
RESULTS QUICKLY

Choir Singers Come to Learn

Everything that is done and said in rehearsal should serve a single purpose—to produce better church music. That's what your singers come for, and that's what they have every right to expect.

The belief that progress can be made only by slow, painstaking methods is simply not true. Correct methods in rehearsal will produce immediate and dramatic improvements in singing; that's why they are the correct methods.

Singers Learn by Doing, not by Lectures

A most important principle of choral rehearsals is that singers learn by doing, not by lectures. In the practice room, the time best invested is the time spent in actual singing. Brief corrections and suggestions are, of course, necessary; rarely, however, should these take more than a few seconds of time.

Out of 60 minutes of rehearsal time, how many minutes do your singers actually sing? Ask someone at your next rehearsal to measure the actual singing time with a stopwatch. If there are 30 minutes of singing out of 60 minutes of rehearsal, half of the rehearsal time is being poorly utilized.

Two basic principles of operation will help to conserve rehearsal time for singing:

a. Eliminate from the rehearsal any activity that can be done at another time; e.g., distributing and retrieving music copies.

b. Resist the temptation to deliver scholarly lectures or personal reminiscences. Give only those instructions that can be put to immediate use.

Illustrate, Don't Orate

The printed page at best gives only a generalized idea of the way music should be performed. Notes, words, marks of expression— these are approximations which you must interpret more precisely for your singers. In rehearsal, even the most distinguished and successful choral directors frequently resort to "rote-teaching," setting patterns and examples for their choirs. They have learned that they can teach music better and faster by using both the ear-gate and the eye-gate. For the ultimate subtle refinements in choral art, there is perhaps no other way.

Whenever possible illustrate what you want by singing, rather than explaining or theorizing. Example is more effective than analysis. Showing is better than telling. Illustrate, don't orate.

Start Precisely on Time

Begin the rehearsal precisely on time, even if the accompanist is not in place and only a few singers are on hand. No matter what time is announced for the rehearsal, some singers will arrive late. It is both unfair and self-defeating to waste the time of those who are punctual, while awaiting the eventual or uncertain arrival of latecomers.

Countering Boredom and Fatigue

Boredom and fatigue are ever-present specters in the rehearsal room; unseen but dangerous. When boredom begins, learning ends.

The most important antidote to boredom is the enthusiasm of the director. Dr. Archibald T. Davison once observed that conducting an amateur chorus was like throwing a rubber ball: the rebound depends upon the force of the throw. Similarly, the response a choral conductor gets from his chorus depends largely upon the energy and enthusiasm of his own effort.

Keep up the momentum of learning.

a. Interesting, worthwhile music to sing is absolutely vital. Everything else depends upon this (p. 98).

b. Change rehearsal activities frequently. Alternate the familiar with the unfamiliar, the easy and the difficult, accompanied and unaccompanied singing.

c. Work no more than ten or 12 minutes at one time on any anthem.

d. Don't always "take it from the top." On some anthems, start at a mid-point, working only on one passage of exceptional difficulty.

e. Encourage quiet singing. This helps the singer to listen to others and forestalls strain and vocal fatigue.

f. Occasionally, remove the rehearsal to another locale. Instead of the choir room, use the sanctuary. Or schedule a rehearsal at some member's home.

g. Insist that some improvement be made each time music is sung. Allow no mindless repetition of a familiar anthem. Always announce a reason for a repetition; set a specific objective. There is no absolute limit to the excellence attainable in choral singing.

h. Keep everyone busy to minimize neighborly chatter or disciplinary problems. While you rehearse one voice-line, have the others hum their parts, or even sing along on the difficult line where practical.

i. In difficult music, teach each voice-line separately; the unisons must be correct before the ensemble can be right.

j. If instruments are to be used in the accompaniment, give the singers plenty of opportunity to get used to their sound in rehearsal.

k. Memorize your scores well enough so that you can move freely about the rehearsal room during the singing. When necessary, move close to, or even into, a voice-section that needs special help.

Correcting Problems . . . One at a Time

Whenever you must stop the choir in rehearsal, you should bring out these points.

a. Explain very briefly why you had to stop them.

b. Demonstrate what must be done to correct the problem.

c. Correct only one thing at a time, no matter how many things are going wrong. Singers generally have difficulty in responding to multiple instructions. Concentrate on the most basic problem. If rhythm, intonation, and diction all need improvement, correct rhythm first, then intonation, then diction.

Isolate, Illustrate, Slow Down, Repeat

The maxim, "Practice Makes Perfect" is at best a half-truth. Only *correct practice* is of real value. The repetition of error without correction is probably more harmful than no practice at all.

Correction of error should thus be made at the earliest practical stage of music-learning; a long-rehearsed error may prove almost impossible to eradicate.

An effective formula for correcting errors in rehearsal is: Isolate . . . Illustrate . . . Slow down . . . Repeat.

a. *Isolate the problem.* Explain precisely what is wrong, and at what measure and beat.

b. *Illustrate the correct procedure.* Pitch and intervals are best illustrated at the piano. Rhythms should be counted, clapped, then sung. Diction should be demonstrated by the director.

c. *Slow down the difficult passage.* If taken slowly enough, the most difficult passage becomes easy (except only extreme range).

d. *Repeat to remember.* To be mastered by the choir, a difficult passage must be reheased—harrowed over—until the last singer in the section (not the best) has it right. Rehearse very slowly until everyone has it right, then work up to performance tempo.

Analyzing Errors and Prescribing Correctives

A conductor needs both inner and outer ears. With an "inner ear," he hears (recalls) the music as it ought to sound. With his "outer ear," he hears the music as it actually sounds. He continuously compares these simultaneous impressions, identifying exactly what is right and what is wrong in the music he hears. He is exercising critical judgement.

A conductor, however, unlike a mere critic, must do more than recognize musical errors; he must also know how to correct them.

a. Correct the error, never the person. Stress positive and constructive action.

Do not say: "You are singing too loudly." This implies a personal criticism.

Do say: "Please sing a true pianissimo, as lightly as this hum." (Demonstrate a hum.)

b. Make a correction with great tact (everyone is supersensitive). Singers genuinely want to please you, if only they understand what you want. Keep loving them, even when they are doing badly. "Whom the Lord loveth, he correcteth . . . " (Proverbs 3:12).

c. Not everyone will comprehend your instructions with equal speed. Be prepared to repeat corrections in slightly different language, or use other illustrations, without becoming impatient.

d. Avoid sarcasm; "tearing the flesh" (its literal meaning) hurts much more than it helps. Correction should be impersonal, humane, and unfailingly good-tempered.

e. Accent the positive. Always try to commend what is well done before you correct what is wrong. Remember that the sole purpose of both praise and correction is to stimulate and encourage the choir to do better work.

f. Whatever your advice, keep it brief.

g. Use specific language whenever possible.

Do say: "Louder . . . faster . . . softer . . . slower." Avoid vague terms that may be misinterpreted, such as "humble . . . prayerful . . . devoutly."

h. Bad sectional tone can usually be improved by quiet singing and by listening to others.

i. Intonation problems often involve a specific interval, such as a minor third which is not accurately sung. Wide intervals (sixths and sevenths) and accidentals are frequently troublesome. When singing goes out of tune, check these most carefully.

Speaking and Reading "Body Talk"

The disciplined conductor is an expert "body talker," communicating very effectively through movements and facial expression. Train your singers to watch closely in rehearsal, and to respond instantly to your conducting signals. Indications of tempo, dynamics, style, tone quality, diction, and such, can be made by signals, without verbal explanation, and without stopping the singing.

A clear and consistent conducting technique can thus become a great time-saver in rehearsal, saving hours that would otherwise be spent on rote-learning and memory-training.

There should, of course, be complete agreement between the interpretative gestures used by the director and the interpretative markings which appear in the music (p.148). Any contradiction will create unnecessary confusion.

Rehearse A Cappella Most of the Time

Piano or organ should be used as little as possible in the church choir rehearsal. Singers who persistently rely on instrumental support never really learn their music. Even the anthems performed with accompaniment should be rehearsed until choristers can sing their parts absolutely independent of instrumental support.

Unaccompanied rehearsal makes the singers listen to each other, rather than to the instrument. They thus become more conscious of the choral sound, rather than of the instrumental sound. The less the instruments are used in rehearsal, the more rapidly will choral tone improve.

A good rule follows: *Music is not ready for public performance until it can be sung confidently without instrumental support.*

Collect and Use Vivid "Ways of Telling"

Experienced directors develop a special lexicon of phrases which summarize their musical ideas in a vivid manner. Some phrases may be original, but most directors collect useful ideas from reading or from watching other directors in action.

When you hear a good phrase, write it down. Memorize it; make it yours. Such phrases may help you explain precisely what you want, without groping for words.

DEVELOPING CHORAL DISCIPLINE

Teaching Musical Literacy

When necessary, the director should teach or review basic musical literacy. At the least, each singer should be able to read note- and rest-values correctly. It is more efficient to teach your singers to count time than it is to teach each new rhythm by rote.

Likewise, much time can be saved if singers know the notes by name. If they develop a reasonably good concept of the frequently sung intervals, the reading of new music can be greatly facilitated.

Writing a Choral Guide

Most choral conductors develop individual methods and routines which they expect their singers to follow. If these are put into writing in the form of a guidebook, the need for repetitious and time-consuming verbal instructions may be greatly reduced.

a. The choral guide can be a simple mimeographed leaflet given to each choir member. Explain clearly the basics of singing: how you want the singer to stand or sit; how to hold the music; how to breathe; the importance of agreeing on the vowel-sound; how to time the consonant more precisely; why he should open his mouth when he sings; why he is expected to watch the director at all times.

b. Occasionally in the rehearsal, discuss or demonstrate one of these points at greater length; encourage questions.

c. If several new members join the choir at one time, the choral guide can be the basis of orientation sessions (p. 66).

On some points of choral singing, successful teachers and directors are sometimes in emphatic disagreement. Perhaps there is more than one "correct" way of standing or breathing. But the director will greatly simplify matters for himself and his singers if he will select one effective method and recommend this to his choristers. Standardized procedures will save a great deal of time in rehearsal.

TEACHING NEW MUSIC TO THE CHOIR

Strive for Total Comprehension of the Music

A step-by-step plan for introducing new music follows.

a. *Explain who-what-when-why.* (60-90 seconds). As the choristers examine the title page of a new octavo, pronounce the composer's name, tell when he lived, and cite, if possible, brief biographical data which explain why and when he wrote this music. Identify the author or source of the text, with any appropriate commentary concerning it.

b. *Identify the nature of the music.* (30 seconds). Point out its literary form: prose or poetry. Identify its dominant mood, or any changes in emotion that occur in the piece.

c. *Read the text aloud as literature.* Where practical, have the choristers read it in unison. If there is a great deal of repetition of phrases, it is best that the director prepare and read aloud a condensed version. Where there are antiphonal passages, let the assigned voices read the part. Encourage clear enunciation at the very first reading.

d. *Clear up obscurities immediately.* Define unusual words or phrases. Clarify questionable pronunciations. Help the choristers to understand the spiritual implications of the text.

e. *Relate the text to the rhythm of the music.* Have the choir read (or chant in monotone) the text aloud a second time, in the rhythm of the music. Solve difficult rhythms immediately.

f. *Let everyone sing the leading melodies.* Have all the choir members sing the melody in unison on a neutral syllable, such as "la" or "loh."

g. *Point out how the composer uses these melodies.* Show the movement of melody from voice to voice. Demonstrate canons, inversions, and other alterations of the basic melodic material.

h. *Join words and notes together, a cappella.* Accustom the singers to "walking alone," without instrumental support, at a very early stage of preparation.

Additional Suggestions. Once the singing has begun, avoid excessive talk or frequent interruptions. Let the music speak for itself.

Reduce larger choral works to logical subsections; it may be very difficult to comprehend an extended work at one sitting, and it is not necessary. Reading new music is very taxing for the singers, physically, mentally, and emotionally. Better to do less at one sitting and have them eager to resume, than to drive them until they are spent and heartily disliking the new piece. Quit while they are still enjoying it.

Permit no full-voice singing on new music.

In reading music, teach the chorister to look ahead, but also to remember where he has been. A phrase often returns to a previously sung note.

Interpretative markings are just as much a part of the music as the words and notes. Insist that singers respond to these from the very first, although the precise degree of response will be refined in later readings.

Learn the Notes or You'll Never Get to the Music

Most bad singing in the church choir can be traced to a single cause: the singers simply do not know the notes. Artistic choral singing is possible only when each member of the ensemble can sing his own part, error-free, solo, and unaccompanied. At your next rehearsal, would you dare to test each of the tenors to see if they could do this?

Individual part-testing is too time consuming to be practical in the church choir. But sectional testing is entirely practical, and you should routinely request that each voice-line "prove" its part by singing it unaccompanied. The SATB choir is basically a blend of four unison voice-lines. Until each individual line (and each individual singer) is correct, there is no real hope of choral excellence or refined musical interpretation.

Spot Rehearsals Make the Rough Places Plain

Troublesome passages must not be glossed over in the vain hope that the errors will just go away or somehow correct themselves. Resolve to make the most difficult measures of each anthem the best-learned and most familiar of all. Concentrate rehearsal effort on these hard spots. When singers feel completely at ease with the more difficult passages, they have the confidence to sing the simpler lines with great style.

RE-DISCOVERING FAMILIAR MUSIC

Nearly every church choir library contains some once-popular anthems that have been reduced to the status of hacks. They have been ridden often and carelessly. Typical of these might be:

- Stainer: "God So Loved the World"
- John Goss: "O Savior of the World"
- MacFarlane: "Open Our Eyes"
- Ivanov: "Bless the Lord, Oh My Soul"

If the performance of these familiars tends to become hackneyed, lead your choristers through an intensive re-study and re-evaluation of the spiritual thought expressed in these great old anthems.

- What does John 3:16 mean to you?
- Do you believe it?
- Why did Stainer have his text set in this form?
- How significant is the recitative which precedes this in the cantata, "The Crucifixion"?

Faith and conviction are the pre-requisites of effective choral communication. As Hugh Roberton, the great English choral conductor and adjudicator, once so wisely observed; "They know not music, who only music know."

Attempts to revitalize the performance of familiar music can be successful only with music of intrinsic worth. Sad to say, many once-popular church anthems simply will not bear close scrutiny;

they are weak theologically, poetically, and musically. Their day has truly passed.

But the genuine classics of religious music possess an inherent and enduring vitality! They have spoken convincingly to succeeding generations of Christians, and they still so speak today. The authentic musical gem glows undimmed by the abrasions of the sands of time. Great music withstands the most intense scrutiny, revealing to the student director ever-new flashes of insight and unsuspected facets of beauty.

It is not we who take the measure of the greatest music; it is, in the end, this music which measures us.

REPRESSION? NO! EXPRESSION? YES!

In the past, it has been the fashion for choristers in performance to appear "cool," emotionally impassive and physically immobile. Many a strong-minded director has disciplined his choir to the point of total conformity and subservience, creating, in the phrase of Charles Ives, an "overdrilled mechanism." Some choirs in performance appear devoid of human feeling, exhibiting not the slightest emotional involvement with their music.

Why should a chorister repress his emotions? Impassivity is not natural to musicians. Soloists almost invariably use facial expression and small gestures to augment the communicative power of song. The top players in a great symphony orchestra are among the most highly disciplined of musicians, yet they are not criticized if they move their bodies in response to the music.

Singing involves more than a larynx; song wells up from one's whole being. If a singer feels emotion, it involves his whole being, and should he not be free to express it with his whole self? Why not let the light shine through . . . at least a little?

9 Producing the Special Program

COUNTING THE COST AND THE CONSEQUENCES

Regular Service Music Is Top Priority

A special music program by the church choir provides an opportunity to present great religious music which cannot be readily accommodated in the usual worship service.

Special musical programs, however, do require a heavy commitment of musical resources and rehearsal time. The director should carefully count the cost (in time and effort) of a special program, in relation to its value in the total church music program.

a. A special program should not be necessary to "hold the interest of the choir." If the regular service music which you have scheduled is all that dull, a radical revision of the basic repertory is much more urgently needed than a one-shot special event.

b. An extra musical event can be justified only when it will not jeopardize the performance of the regular service music. Cantatas and oratorios seem to demand an inordinate amount of rehearsal time, which is taken away from the regular service music. A series of poorly prepared anthems is a high price to pay for one cantata.

Securing Support from Choir and Administration

Before attempting any special musical program, discuss the proposed project with your choir members to determine the extent of their interest and support. In some congregations, evening oratorios have long been traditional. But it is apparent that in many localities, public support for these events has been diminishing.

If the choristers are generally in favor, consult with the pastor and church music committee. It is not wise to attempt an ambitious musical evening without the solid backing of the administration.

171

SPECIAL PROGRAMS IN THE HOME CHURCH

Choosing a Time for the Program

Christmas and Easter are the traditional times for special church musical programs, because interest in religious affairs is normally high at these periods. Counter-poised to this natural advantage is the fact that these are already peak periods in the choir's workload. The added rehearsals necessary to prepare a major musical program may be a heavy burden at these times. Then too, other church choirs, plus school and community choral groups, will all be vying for an audience in the crowded holiday calendar.

Consider the possibilities of a special musical program at an off-peak period. There are numerous religious festivals and obser- vances when a program might be most appropriate:

- Reformation Day (October 31).
- All Saints' Day (November 1).
- Thanksgiving Day (Late November).
- Last Sunday in Trinity (5 weeks before Christmas).
- Presentation of Our Lord (February 2).
- First Sunday in Lent (6 weeks before Easter).
- Cantate Sunday (4th Sunday after Easter).
- Ascension of Our Lord (40 days after Easter).
- Pentecost; Whitsunday (7th Sunday after Easter).
- Festival of Holy Trinity (8th Sunday after Easter).

There is an abundance of excellent music which can be used appropriately on such occasions.

Selecting Music for the Special Program

The presentation of an oratorio, cantata, Mass, or Passion will involve a substantial financial investment, in addition to the expendi- ture of time and energy. Invest your resources in the very best; don't waste money and effort on mediocre, superficial stuff.

a. A major musical work must inspire the genuine interest of the church choir and the *public of today*. Most of the once-popular 19th century cantatas simply have not stood the test of time. If you expect people to leave their TV sets and stereos to attend your performance, your music must have something to say to the churchgoer of today. Few listeners will willingly submit to two hours of tedium.

b. The music must be completely within the capacity of your performers. The average parish choir simply is not up to Bach's "St. Matthew Passion" or "B Minor Mass." Do not attempt an oratorio if you don't have really outstanding soloists available; "Elijah" is no role for your garden-variety baritone.

c. Use the original accompaniment wherever possible. Most, if not all, major choral works were written to be accompanied with an instrumental ensemble, rather than keyboard instruments. Even a modest string ensemble can greatly brighten a performance of Bach, Handel, Haydn, Vivaldi, Mozart, Schubert, et alii. Classic and Romantic religious works which call for a full symphony orchestra can seldom be well performed by a church choir (Beethoven: "Missa Solemnis," Brahms: "German Requiem," Verdi: "Requiem," etc.). The instrumental resources available in the typical church simply aren't adequate.

Special organ adaptations of the orchestral score are available for Handel's "Messiah" and perhaps a few other choral works. These are better than the keyboard reduction found in the choral score, but certainly less effective than even a small instrumental ensemble.

d. Excepting Handel's "Messiah," few great religious choral works were originally written to English texts. The English versions are all translations, and vary considerably in their sense and singability. Compare various editions of the popular Bach cantatas or the great Mass settings before making a choice.

e. Many major choral works contain at least two or three choruses which would be useful additions to the choir's repertory of Sunday anthems. In selecting music for the special programs, give preference to that which can be doubly useful in the regular worship service.

Minor Masterworks of Church Music

A practical alternative to the special evening choir program is the use of minor (shorter) choral masterworks which can be presented within the time-frame of a regular worship service. Most pastors will approve a cantata lasting five to ten minutes, or a festive setting of the Mass or liturgy.

Originally, the term "cantata" simply designated the principal choral music to be sung in the worship service. In J.S. Bach's day, the cantata occupied 20 to 30 minutes of a four-hour church service. In the present day, a cantata of five to ten minutes would seem to be in reasonable proportion to the rest of the service.

Choral masterworks of this duration have been produced in nearly every period of music history. The list of available works grows each year with new editions of older music and many contemporary compositions. The possibilities are limited only by the research and musical imagination of the church music director.

Massed Choirs; Hymn Festivals; Oratorio Reading

Choirs from neighboring congregations may combine to present a church music festival. This could be a hymn festival, a choir festival, or a combination of these. Such a festival requires little additional rehearsal for each participating choir, but does demand superb organization and management.

a. The organizing committee should include the music directors of each participating choir. The director of the host church is a logical choice as chairman. Each committee member should be assigned to a specific function: publicity, program compiling and printing, seating, refreshments, social activities, etc.

b. A practical festival format allows each choir to sing one or two selections on its own. As a finale, all singers combine into a massed chorus for two or three selections, perhaps with special instrumental accompaniment. Choirs which normally wear vestments should do so in the festival.

c. For massed chorus work, make certain that all choirs are using absolutely identical versions of the music, whether hymns or sacred choruses. Even slight variations in text, melody, or harmony can cause confusion if not consternation in the performance. Each choir should have the correct music copies at least five weeks before the festival.

d. Assign each choir to a specific seating location in the auditorium. Reserve only the actual seats required for each choir, as space may be at a premium.

e. Personality problems are sometimes eased if the combined massed chorus is directed by an outside guest.

f. An organ solo or other instrumental music may provide welcome contrast in an otherwise all-choral program.

g. A social mixer before or after the program gives singers from the various churches an opportunity to become acquainted.

h. A suggested timetable for a Sunday-evening festival:

- 4:15 p.m.　　Choirs assemble at the host church.
　　　　　　　　Find assigned seating locations.

- 4:30 p.m.   Announcements. Introductions. Instructions.
- 4:45 p.m.   Rehearse massed chorus; guest conductor.
- 6:00 p.m.   Pot-luck supper. Social hour.
- 7:15 p.m.   Choir members robe and prepare for program.
- 7:30 p.m.   Festival begins.

i. Something to remember in planning is: with a large number of choirs participating, there may be very little space for an audience. Count carefully.

Oratorio Reading. An interesting development in choral singing is the oratorio reading. This gives choristers the pleasure of singing great music without the necessity of perfecting it for the public performance.

Organizers provide an auditorium, a distinguished conductor, competent professional soloists, and instrumental accompaniment. Singers pay a small fee to defray the expense, and each provides his own copy of the work to be sung. Participants should have worked out their parts at home so they will not be sight-reading.

The reading is conducted as a performance; there are no stops for corrections or improvements. In some instances, authoritative comments about the music (historical notes, etc.) are well received.

SPECIAL PROGRAMS AWAY FROM HOME

Concerts at Institutions and Missions

Choristers sometimes find a special satisfaction in singing away from the familiar home church. Visiting choirs may be welcomed by mission congregations, retirement or convalescent homes, community centers, and corrective institutions. An inquiry from your pastor addressed to the chaplain or director of the institution will provide the initial contact.

Singing away from home entails little or no additional rehearsal time. A suitable program can usually be selected from current repertory.

a. Agree with the institutional officer in charge on an exact date, hour, and location for the choral program. Exchange memoranda, confirming everything in writing.

b. Many institutions have very limited auditorium facilities, and some have none at all. Visit the proposed concert site in person, long in advance of the appearance, to determine how best to utilize the existing facilities. Perhaps there will be no piano or organ available, or an instrument so badly out of tune as to be useless. This will certainly have an effect on the repertory you select and the instruments you will bring.

c. Give each choir member a written resumé of the arrangements, summarizing all pertinent facts. It is best to solicit the signatures of all members on a "go" or "no go" basis (p. 73).

d. Delegate responsibility for transportation arrangements. Car pools are a practical solution in many cases. If robes are to be used, let each singer be responsible for his own. Librarians should look after the transportation, distribution, and retrieval of music copies. The director should bring his own stand and podium.

e. The inmates of a prison, mental hospital, or home for the aged may not react to the music in the polite and usually passive manner of your conventional churchgoer. It is well to forewarn the singers of this possibility.

Singing at Other Churches

If your home church has no afternoon or evening service, there may be others which do, and these might welcome the appearance of a visiting choir.

In the vacation months, churches near recreational areas sometimes sponsor religious services in campgrounds. A church choir which is off-duty in its home church can add much to these usually informal exercises.

Radio, Television, Recordings

Singing for re-broadcast via electronic media is vastly different from singing a live performance in your home church. Despite substantial advances in sound-recording techniques, at the present state-of-the-art, none do full justice to choral sound. When recording, one must adjust to this reality. In most instances, best results are attained by restricting the dynamic range to rather narrow limits, approximately mp to mf. Only the most advanced professional recording setups will handle Brucknerian ppp or FFF.

a. *Music for radio or TV:* This kind of music must be performed with meticulous care. These media are extremely faithful in exposing—no, emphasizing—every choral fault or weakness. Most choirs sound best in homophonic pieces; complex polyphony or counterpoint seldom survives the recording process as well.

The well-run broadcasting studio will provide the director with explicit instructions preparatory to the recording or taping session. It will make things easier for all if these are followed to the letter. The station will also request an advance listing of all music selections in order to obtain the necessary performance rights.

b. *Custom-recording.* Professional or semi-professional sound-recording service is now widely available. Almost any church choir which so desires can make an LP or stereo recording. Either on-site or in-studio recording service may be available; they come to you or you go to them. Studio recordings entail more trouble and travel for the choir, but are generally somewhat superior. Better equipment is likely to be used at the studio, and acoustical conditions may be better controlled.

The church choir should not expect spectacular results in these ventures. Large groups of voices are difficult to record under the best of circumstances, with the finest of special equipment. Few local studios possess either the sophisticated technical equipment or the necessary engineering skill. Further, the typical parish choir just doesn't perform at the level of professional perfection we hear on commercial recordings. Nonetheless, a recording of the church choir usually excites the interest of the choristers and their families and friends in the congregation.

If the recording is to be sold, make certain that you obtain from the publishers the performance right for all copyrighted material.

ORGANIZING A MAJOR MUSICAL PRODUCTION

Inventory the Required Musical Resources

In preparing an oratorio, Mass, or cantata, the first step is an inventory of the musical resources which will be required. This should be comprehensive and itemized in specific detail.

Soloists. List the numbers which each will sing. Don't overlook the "bit parts" in many dramatic works which require a solo voice.

Instrumental Accompaniment. Whenever possible, use the composer's original instrumentation in preference to the keyboard reduction. List each instrument required and the number of players you plan to use on each part: four first violins, three second violins, three violas, etc.

Chorus Work. Carefully time the duration of each chorus you plan to include. In your planning, allow at least 30 minutes of rehearsal time for each minute of chorus performance.

Copies. These should be ordered at once. Long delays in

delivery are not uncommon, and can seriously upset your whole production timetable. If choral scores or instrumental parts are to be rented, reserve these as early as possible to assure availability, even if delivery is requested for a much later date.

Engaging Soloists and Instrumentalists

Good soloists are particularly important in an oratorio, and the director owes it to the chorus to hire the best he can find. The chorus will have to work very hard to get their parts ready, and it is certainly disheartening to them if their performance is jeopardized by shaky solo work.

The safe procedure is to hire only experienced professional soloists. Music department personnel in a nearby college may provide excellent leads. And often, when one soloist has been engaged, he can suggest others whom he knows to be competent.

Music schools and colleges may also recommend rising young singers who have an interest in oratorio work. There is more risk in hiring these than in hiring the established professional. But even the greatest singers have to start somewhere, and your choir may long remember the excitement of hearing a young artist who later achieves fame on the operatic or concert stage.

The best soloists are usually booked early, so it is good business to contact them as soon as you have affirmed a date for the performance. When approaching a professional singer, either directly, or through a manager, give the entire picture before you ask for a decision:

- What will be performed.
- Where.
- When: both date and hour.
- Rehearsal arrangements.
- What you can afford to pay.

Most soloists are somewhat flexible about fees for a non-profit church engagement. If you are hiring several soloists, as for the "Messiah," offer all the same fee. You will build considerable resentment if any soloists discover preferential treatment.

After a soloist accepts, confirm all details of the engagement and verify the fee in a personal note. Provide each soloist with a copy of the Project Guide (p. 179) as soon as this is available. Request from each soloist publicity material and pictures. Publicity is important to a professional singer, and it is important to the success of your performance (see Publicizing the Program below).

By definition, a professional sings for money, and he will appreciate prompt payment. Whenever practical, arrange to present payment at the time of the performance.

Instrumentalists. It is frequently necessary to augment a congregational orchestra by engaging outside players. These may be local townspeople, or students in nearby high schools or colleges. Contact them as early as possible; recruiting an orchestra seems very easy to postpone.

If the orchestra will comprise more than a dozen players, appoint an orchestra manager. He can relieve you of many time-consuming organizational details: recruiting personnel, notifying players of rehearsals, responsibility for the instrumental copies, etc.

Compiling the Project Guide

When all arrangements have been completed for the special program, compile and publish a Project Guide. This summarizes important information about the performance, and a copy should be provided for everyone who may be involved in any way: soloists, chorus members, instrumentalists, pastor, music committee, chief usher, building custodian, church office, publicity people. The Project Guide confirms:

- Title of work, composer, edition used.
- Name of church, address, office phone.
- Date and hour of performance.
- Name, address, and phone number of each soloist, the director, accompanists, the orchestra manager.
- Size of chorus and orchestra.
- Dress (vestments) for soloists, chorus, orchestra.
- Rehearsal times for soloists, orchestra, chorus.
- Exact selections to be performed (portions of longer works are frequently omitted).
- Who performs and who accompanies each selection.
- Personnel of the chorus and orchestra may be listed on a supplemental sheet.

Publicizing the Program

It sometimes requires as much effort to get people to attend a special choral program as it does to produce it. An audience has a very direct bearing upon the performance; singers are stimulated by a full house and discouraged at the prospect of singing to empty pews.

Good publicity can help to fill the church, and should be carefully planned from the very outset of the project. An active publicity committee should be in operation at the inception of rehearsals. Each member of the committee should be assigned to specific publicity media:

- Announcements in church.
- Notices in church publications.
- Posters and handbills.
- Direct mail: invitations, announcements, etc.
- Community newspapers: pictures and stories.
- Local radio and TV.
- Personal phone solicitation.

In addition to building an audience, a strong publicity campaign also builds morale among the performers; the program is made to seem increasingly important. Good publicity also builds the prestige of the church in the eyes of the community, which most pastors will deem desirable.

Provide a Helpful Program

A printed program for the performance can be of real assistance to the audience. At the least, it should list what is being sung, and by whom. In addition, a synopsis of the story, or a précis of the text, will be much appreciated.

If the singing is in Latin, German, or another language unfamiliar to the audience, an English translation is almost a necessity.

Concise program notes and biographical data are generally appreciated, but please avoid the musicological jargon of big-time music critics or program annotators. In a church bulletin, program notes should aim to be genuinely helpful, not academically impressive.

Delegating Ancillary Functions

A smoothly run musical program requires the close coordination of many non-musical functions and services. The music director usually has about all he can do to prepare his musicians for the performance, and should delegate all possible ancillary functions to others. It is a mistake to attempt a "one-man show."

Stage preparation should be supervised by the building custo-dian. He should have the assistance of ushers or choir men in setting up risers, chairs for the performers, or any other special equipment required.

Printed programs can usually be handled through the church office. The copy, including program notes, should be prepared by the director, or at least checked by him.

Ushering should be handled by the regular staff.

Lighting requires an experienced person familiar with the electrical controls in the auditorium. For his guidance, provide a specially marked copy of the program, clearly indicating all lighting cues and changes. Be sure that lighting is adequate wherever congregational participation (as in hymns) is expected.

Decorations, including flowers, can be very helpful in establishing an appropriate mood for the program. Use seasonal motifs wherever possible. The ladies' Altar Guild or other groups are usually most cooperative in working out a suitable decor.

PREPARING THE MUSICIANS

Rehearse Each Component Separately

A cardinal principle in preparing a large-scale musical work is: *divide and conquer.* The majority of large-scale works employ three components: chorus, soloists, and orchestra. Each of these elements should be individually prepared before any combined rehearsals are attempted. It is terribly inefficient to have an orchestra sitting idly by while the chorus struggles with its notes, or vice versa.

The rehearsal accompanist should receive a score of the oratorio (Mass, cantata) as soon as it has been selected. It is well worthwhile to have this copy especially bound with hinged tape, plastic comb, or wire spiral so that the pages will stay open. Director and accompanist should carefully review the score together, writing in exact metronomic tempi and agreeing on the interpretative markings. If available, a phonograph recording may be of great assistance in these initial studies. Long before the first rehearsal with the chorus, director and accompanist should feel thoroughly comfortable with the work as a whole, and be familiar with every important detail. Both should understand how the finished performance ought to sound.

The experienced soloist will insist on rehearsal with the orches-tra or accompanist, no matter how many times he has previously sung his role. He will not run unnecessary risks with his hard-won reputation. Where solo and chorus work are closely coordinated, plan joint rehearsals at least three weeks prior to performance; this allows time to correct errors.

The orchestra is often the weak component in oratorio performances. The typical oratorio orchestra has had much less rehearsal than the chorus. While they may get through without a major collapse, oratorio orchestras generally lack the polish and finesse of the highly trained chorus or experienced soloist.

The cure for this is obviously more rehearsal time. But, where players are professionals, the cost of extra rehearsals may be prohibitive. And, even amateur players are sometimes so busy that extra rehearsals are almost impossible to arrange. For the best possible preparation of the players, try these suggestions.

a. Get the instrumental parts to the players as early as practical. Order a separate part for each player. On rented scores, this may mean paying a small additional rental fee for extra parts and extra time. Be sure that all "cuts" or changes are correctly and clearly indicated in each part. Encourage individual practice.

b. In most scores, it will pay to have a string sectional. Wind and percussion players rightly resent sitting by with nothing to do while strings are ironing out their technical difficulties.

c. Start orchestra rehearsals early in the preparation period. This will expose the difficulties of the players who have not individually practiced their parts and give them time to make amends.

d. Schedule at least one full rehearsal with orchestra, chorus, and soloists.

Choral conductors are often criticized (and justly) by instrumental players as being erratic, vague, and difficult to follow. There is nothing gained by trying to argue the point; if the players have trouble following your beat, your performance is going to suffer. Use standard, internationally accepted conducting movements. This will save much rehearsal time and greatly reduce the chances of misunderstanding and misinterpretation.

In rehearsal, and in performance as well, remember to conduct not just the chorus but also the orchestra. The choral conductor may be used to working with an accompanist so sensitive that she can practically read his mind. The orchestra cannot read your mind; it requires attention, instruction, and competent direction.

Finding Extra Rehearsal Time

It is almost certain that a special program cannot be added to the choir's normal activities without somehow increasing the rehearsal time.

a. Reduce the choir's workload of regular service music. Schedule fewer anthems, or easier, familiar anthems. Begin preparation of a major work at least ten to 12 weeks in advance of performance. Budget 30 to 50% of each regular rehearsal period to the special program.

b. It may be practical to gain additional rehearsal time by extending the normal rehearsal period by 15 to 30 minutes each week. Start earlier or finish later than usual. Do this only with the previous assent of the choir.

c. Encourage special sectional rehearsals at choir-members' homes. These can be pleasant semi-social get-togethers. "Singing along" with a stereo recording of the work at a sectional rehearsal can be good fun, and instructional, too.

d. If extra rehearsals appear necessary, these should be scheduled and announced at the inception of the project. It is unfair, and should be unnecessary, to call emergency extra rehearsals as a last-ditch effort to "save the performance."

Controlling the Choir's Workload

a. Don't let the choir become dismayed by the appearance of a bulky choral score, such as Mendelssohn's "Elijah." In many major works, a comparatively small portion of the total may be for the chorus. It is often more practical for a church choir to present portions of a major work, or a condensed version, than to attempt the entire opus.

b. In 18th century cantatas, some movements can as well be sung by a quartette as by a chorus, and it is sometimes difficult to tell the composer's true intention. Of the eight sections in J.S. Bach's great cantata #80, "A Mighty Fortress Is Our God," only #1 and #5 need be done by chorus. Others could be done by soloists or unison sections; the concluding chorale could be for congregation and/or chorus. Thus, the work of the chorus can be adjusted by assigning sections to solo voices.

c. In Masses, it is not always necessary to sing the Credo;

liturgically, it is not required. Many settings of the Mass do not provide music for the Credo at all. So if it is necessary to reduce the choir's work, consider omitting a difficult Credo.

Check Every Detail in the Final Rehearsals

Schedule at least two rehearsals when the entire work will be read without interruption or correction. The first of these complete readings should be about four weeks prior to the performance. This will give everyone an opportunity to assess his personal progress.

The Dress Rehearsal. This should be held two weeks prior to the performance. It should not include musicians only, but everyone involved in the staging of the production. The dress rehearsal two weeks before performance allows time for correction of problems.

Seating the Chorus and Orchestra. Prepare and post a seating chart in advance, assigning a specific place to each participant. Waste no precious rehearsal time on this, nor trust to luck. Appoint an "assistant in charge of seating problems"; make sure he understands what you want, and let him expedite everything at both the rehearsal and performance.

In arranging seating, be as considerate of each chorister as you are of each soloist; satisfactory seating is important to every participant. Choristers should be comfortably spaced, never cramped nor crowded. Be sure that each can see the conductor and hear the other voices and instruments.

Choreographics. Practice the entrance and exit of the choir (processional? recessional?). Teach the quiet way to stand up and sit down: feet flat on the floor before rising or sitting. Remind the chorus not to turn pages with the soloists.

Lighting. House lights and chancel (stage) light should be used in the dress rehearsal exactly as in the performance.

Microphones. Electronic amplification should never be used in choral works. Make certain that *all* microphones are "off" during the rehearsal and performance.

Accompaniment. Make sure that all keyboard instruments are properly tuned to A=440. Check organ registration, if that instrument will be used with the orchestra.

Soloists. These singers should be placed on the platform where they can be heard to best advantage. This is usually in front of the orchestra (not behind nor within). Make certain that each soloist can see the director and the accompanist clearly.

PRESENTING THE SPECIAL PROGRAM

Don't Leave Your Performance on the Floor of the Rehearsal Room

Before assembling the choir on performance night, set up in the rehearsal room a facsimile of the platform seating. This will avoid much confusion and permits last-minute adjustment in the seating plan.

The chorus should be in place about 45 minutes before performance time. In the last minutes, do everything possible to build confidence in the singers, and to create an air of anticipation and excitement.

The time for hard rehearsing is past; strenuous singing at this point is a serious mistake. Tired voices and nervous singers won't make good music. *Don't leave your performance on the floor of the rehearsal room.* Tune up and warm up the singers. Let them sing a portion of each chorus lightly and a cappella, as a tantalizing "preview."

Most of all, get the singers to think about the meaning and message in the music they are about to sing. Get them in the mood of the music, ready to experience and express everything that the composer intended.

After the Performance

Much remains for the director to do after a special program. The project is not complete until these final details are cared for.

Librarians should recover all choral scores and instrumental parts at once. These are costly if lost, and in some cases, almost impossible to replace.

Special stage setups should be cleared promptly. Arrange for extra hands to help the building custodian in this work.

Send "thank you" notes to any who have helped make the program a success; especially to those who have worked behind the scenes, out of the public eye. Let them know you appreciate what they have done.

Retain All Records for Reference

Retain in a special large-capacity filing envelope:

• A roster of chorus and orchestra.

- Correspondence with soloists.
- Copies of the Project Guide (p. 179).
- Church bulletins with announcements.
- Program for the performance.
- Posters, handbills, tickets, invitations.
- Newspaper clippings: publicity and reviews.
- Advertising copy.
- Pictures.

These records will prove invaluable in the event of a repeat performance in later years.

Assessing Public Response

Check the attendance and financial figures for the program; most church offices maintain such records. Compare these with previous programs of earlier years. The real objectives of church programs are, of course, spiritual and artistic rather than numerical. But numbers do provide one index of public response and may serve as a useful guide in planning future programs.

10 Sing to the Lord!

MUSIC IN CHURCH; IT'S DIFFERENT

"... To the Glory of God Alone"

We are told that J.S. Bach inscribed his manuscripts "Soli Deo Gloria"–"To the Glory of God Alone." It might be a useful reminder of basic purpose if we church musicians followed this example, and, along with other interpretative markings, wrote on the title page of each anthem: "To the Glory of God Alone."

Music in church *is* different from music in the secular world. Religious music is not performed for personal glory, but for the glory of God. It may be that we need the humility and dedication of J.S. Bach as much as we need his music.

The Director Sets the Style

As director of a church choir, you are a spiritual leader as well as a musical technician. Your involvement in the worship service ought to be personal and spiritual, as well as professional and musical. Your attitude, for good or ill, sets a mode of behavior which singers note carefully and tend to follow. If you are reverent and attentive, your singers are likely to follow your good example.

PRE-PERFORMANCE WARM-UP IS IMPERATIVE

Making the Final Adjustments

The director should arrive at the rehearsal room about 45 minutes before the start of the worship service. The singers should arrive about 30 minutes before the service. The extra 15 minutes will allow the director to check on the rehearsal facilities and music, and carefully examine the service bulletin for the day. This latter procedural step is especially important, in view of unanticipated changes in the service or errors in the printing. It certainly helps if the director and organist are fully aware of what is going to happen in the service.

Established Routines Conserve Time

A singer should be in place and ready for rehearsal within 60 seconds of his arrival at the rehearsal room, if vestments and music distribution are well-routinized. The printed service bulletins should be stacked where singers can get them as they pick up their anthem folios and hymnals.

Choristers are mostly sociable folk who enjoy the conversation of friends. Small talk can consume large amounts of precious rehearsal time. Encourage singers to find their places quickly; suggest that they visit after church.

Changes in the service or important announcements should be written on the chalkboard for all to see. It is good insurance to read the really important items to the choir before they leave the rehearsal room. Busy people tend to overlook or forget details, however important.

Adjusting Seating and Choral Balance

Seating in the warm-up rehearsal should be a facsimile of that in the choir loft. The placement of voices in each section will have a vital effect on the sound of the choir, and should be deliberately managed by the director, not left to chance (p. 66). Disperse the strong, leading voices throughout each voice section.

If there is a soloist in the anthem, arrange for him to stand well apart from the choir, and preferably in front of the other voices.

Maintain a Relaxed and Pleasant Atmosphere

Despite the inevitable problems and pressures which seem ever-present at the Sunday morning warm-up, try to maintain a pleasant and serene attitude. If you are tense and up-tight, the singers will soon reflect this. The human voice instantly and accurately reveals emotional stress or physical fatigue. Harsh criticism or hard-driving rehearsal methods will likely destroy all hope of beautiful singing.

The warm-up period is no place for major technical corrections. Help the singers concentrate on the text and the message of the anthem to be sung; help them get into the mood of the music. Most texts reflect the Word of God; there is power in that Word, and you can rely on it to touch hearts, minds, and spirits. Just before service, a quiet time or simple prayer may help bring everyone together in the Spirit.

CHOIR CHOREOGRAPHY: PROCESSIONS AND SUCH

" . . . Marching as to War . . . ?"

In some church auditoriums, a formal procession affords the most orderly and practical way to move the singers in and out of the choir loft. Even where other access and egress is possible, some clergymen favor ecclesiastical processions as a dramatic way to begin and end the worship service. But processions can present a raggle-taggle appearance unless well done.

a. The organ console is often located at some distance from the starting point of the procession. It is obviously awkward if the organist begins the processional hymn before the choir and clergy have assembled in the narthex or foyer. Synchronized watches will provide approximate coordination. But for safety, arrange that a definite "go" -signal be given to the organist when the procession is fully formed and ready to move.

b. Processionals can be walked or marched in step. Marching presents a more organized and disciplined aspect, but, to some eyes, seems somewhat militaristic. If the choir does march in step, count two pulses to the measure—left foot on "one," right foot on "two." The organist must count precisely two pulses (steps) between stanzas or chaos will result as the singers shuffle their feet, trying to get back in rhythm.

In either marching or walking, choristers should hold shoulder-sway to a minimum.

c. Sing the processional and recessional hymns in unison. If the choir sings in parts, the man-in-the-pew hears fragments of each passing voice-line; this affords little useful support or leadership for congregational participation.

The Choreography of Worship

In many worship rituals, there are times when it is proper for the congregation to sit, to stand, to kneel, to bow, to make the sign of the cross, or to turn to the altar. If the choir is visible to the congregation, they are the natural leaders in the simple choreography of worship. Because they are leaders, it is advisable that they rehearse the movements of ritual as they rehearse the musical responses.

CONDUCTING THE CHOIR IN THE WORSHIP SERVICE

Invisibility: A Dubious Tradition

A tradition lingers in some churches dictating that the choir director should by some means be made invisible to the congregation. This has often meant that the director is not completely visible to his choir, either. Some hide behind a corner or strategically placed panel, trying to conduct with the aid of mirrors. Others stand at one end of the choir, pretending to sing (or worse, actually singing), trying to hold things together with a nod of the head or wave of the music folio.

This quaint and peculiar notion, without a shred of Scriptural support or liturgical validity, remains a needless and irrational barrier to choral progress. It is no more "incorrect" for the church choir director to be visible during the singing of an anthem than it is "incorrect" for the pastor to be visible during the delivery of the sermon. Both are (or ought to be) communicating important and inspirational ideas; both are more effective (or ought to be) when they can be seen as well as heard.

The finest professional orchestras and choruses, rehearsed to perfection, employ a fully visible conductor to help them perform at their best. The parish choir with less-experienced personnel, and much less rehearsal time, is surely entitled to no less assistance in performance. The right place for a choral conductor in church or elsewhere is directly in front of his choir. He must have eye-to-eye contact with his singers.

The visible director, however, ought to conduct with great restraint, in a way that is not distracting to the worshippers. Choral conducting in church demands enormous self-discipline. Frantic arm-waving is as inappropriate as it is unnecessary; teach the singers to respond to a "vest pocket" beat. Keep your hands directly in front of your body, at shoulder height, so that singers in one glance can take in both your hand signals and facial expression.

Good form in conducting is largely the elimination of waste motion.

The Conductor Is the Pivot-Point of Performance

Performance is the "moment of truth" for the director and the choir alike. In performance, singers are utterly dependent upon the conductor. He is the core (heart) (center) of his choir. No matter how well the choristers know their parts, if the conductor fails or falters, all will follow. The conductor is the axis upon which all else turns. He must be absolutely stable and true; the singers must know that they can rely upon him implicitly.

The director should conduct a perfect performance, even if his chorus is less than perfect. He must know what the music says and what he should be hearing from his performers at every instant. His indications must be precise, his intentions unmistakably clear to the performers. His slightest uncertainty or ambiguity will be instantly reflected in the singing.

Get Up . . . Get Set . . . Go!

A musical performance begins, not with the first note, but at the moment the director steps before his ensemble.

a. Every chorister should have his music open and ready before the conductor appears; no last-second folio fumbling.

b. When the director steps to the podium, he should be looking directly at his singers; every eye in the choir should immediately contact his.

c. All rise upon signal from the director.

d. Allow a few seconds after they rise for the singers to get physically poised and mentally adjusted to the mood of the piece. Keep scanning the choir to make certain that the singers farthest away from you are as ready as those in front. Your mien should cue the mood of the music; no beamish smile as a prelude to "O Sacred Head Now Wounded."

e. If the anthem is to be sung unaccompanied, signal for the opening pitch. Each singer confirms the pitch by sounding it "mentally," or in the lightest possible hum. A hum audible to the congregation is too loud.

f. At this point, some directors find it helpful to close their eyes, shutting out all distractions, and get into the music by mentalizing the opening phrase exactly as it should be performed. The choir remains raptly attentive during these few seconds.

g. Totally absorbed in the music, the director then raises his hands to signal "Get set!" The preparatory "breath beat" and the initial attack follow immediately. Do not hold the choir on "Get set," as their intense concentration before the attack is impossible to sustain for very long. The "breath beat" should clearly indicate the tempo, the dynamic, and the mood of the music to follow.

h. If there is an instrumental introduction to the anthem, the starting sequence for the players is parallel to that for the singers. If the organ only plays the introduction, the director can simply nod to the organist when the choir is ready, and indicate the tempo in an inconspicuous manner. Do not "conduct" the organist; pick up the beat for the choir a few measures before their entrance.

i. It is helpful if the singers are taught to memorize at least the first few notes of each anthem, so that they can give you their total attention at the instant of attack.

Conducting to Create Confidence and Security

a. Perform the anthem exactly as you have rehearsed it. Never attempt impromptu changes in interpretation. Singers can learn nothing new during a performance; at best they can demonstrate what you have previously taught (or failed to teach) them.

b. *Do not sing with your choir.* The singing conductor is prevented by the sound of his own voice from hearing what his choir is really doing. He may think he can hear, and this is a dangerous illusion. Further, a conductor with an outstanding voice is usually just that . . . outstanding, when he ought not to be. It is virtually impossible for a conductor to give equal attention to all voice-lines while singing one of them.

c. Mouthing the words soundlessly is a sometimes effective way of reminding the singers to strengthen their diction. Continual mouthing can become an annoying and occasionally ludicrous mannerism. And if mouthing is used as a substitute for a clear conducting technique, it is downright obnoxious.

d. Good choral conducting is an invitation to make beautiful music. The best conductors maintain an inner serenity and calm, which performers find encouraging and inspiring. The angry countenance and aggressive gesture serve no useful purpose in choral conducting. Choristers can be led to the heights of music, but they cannot be driven there.

e. *Empathy between conductor and singers must be total.* The good conductor experiences everything that he expects of his singers, excepting only the actual production of sound. He breathes with them, mentalizes pitches, vowels, consonants, dynamic changes, phrases. As he does so, each of these details finds expression in his conducting.

When You Sing "Credo," You'd Better Believe It!

a. *Emotionalized singing.* Choral tone faithfully reveals the emotions of the choristers. If the Kyrie ("Lord, have mercy") of the liturgical mass is sung with the same spirit and voice-quality as the Gloria ("Glory to God in the highest"), the singers have somehow missed the very essence of the music, no matter how expertly they perform the notes. The absence of real emotion and personal involvement perhaps accounts for the lack of conviction which is a pervasive weakness of choral ensembles. Too many choirs sing notes instead of songs. In Arturo Toscanini's phrase, they have: "Too much in the head, not enough in the heart."

Singers must understand and feel before they express music effectively. If they are to unite in song, they must first unite in mind and spirit. Each must think, not of himself, but of the message to be shared.

When singers are truly "in the Spirit," everything about their singing is transformed. When emotions such as joy, sorrow, love, and compassion are deeply felt, they affect the singer's posture, breathing, and facial expression. But most important of all, emotions control the tone of his voice. Our inmost feelings are faithfully portrayed or betrayed by our voice. In a telephone conversation, though you cannot see the other party, you can readily tell if he is smiling or scowling, if he is confident or apprehensive. Invariably, we accept the tone of his voice as a much more reliable indication of his feelings than the actual words which are spoken.

It is so in choral singing. Without true joy in the heart, a "hallelujah" sung is no "hallelujah" at all.

b. *Emotionalized conducting.* In choral singing, the director is the most deeply involved of all participants. He experiences to the fullest, the mood and meaning of the music, and he helps his singers experience these, too. If the anthem is a prayer, it is *his* prayer; if it is a song of praise, *his* heart should leap for joy. Truly religious music is to be experienced and deeply felt, not merely mouthed or mimed.

A worshipping congregation hungers for the Word of God, not for the sound of the choir. But, when things are right, the Word of God can be set forth by the choir with a beauty and power that reach far beyond speech alone.

What to Do if Things Go Wrong

There is a "Murphy's Law" of scientific research which states: "Anything that can go wrong *will* go wrong." This law applies equally well to musical performances. Nearly every church choir director can tell of accidents or weird happenings:

- Birds fly into church.
- Car brakes squeal; cars crash during anthems.

- Babies start to cry.
- Organs cypher or lose wind power.
- Choristers become faint or ill.
- Trains whistle and air horns blast during the most solemn moments.
- Planes roar overhead.
- Microphones unaccountably begin to squawk.

Untoward events can be very distracting to the choir and congregation. To minimize their effect, the director must remain outwardly unperturbed, absorbed in the music, oblivious to the distraction. If you show alarm or become distracted, you will surely trigger the disintegration of your performance.

If a disturbance occurs before the choir has begun to sing, wait it out; most disruptions will quickly pass or be corrected.

"Thanks . . . Well Sung!"

The psychologist, William James, pointed out that one of the deepest hungers of the human heart is the hunger for appreciation. Church choristers usually try their very best to sing as you have taught them. In return, they ask only appreciation and encouragement.

At the close of an anthem, hold the choir still for a few seconds. In these fleeting moments, each chorister is asking with his eyes, "How did we do?" If they have done well, tell them so with a slight smile or nod, a private signal that says "Thanks . . . well sung!"

Of course there are times when the director may wish things had gone better; few musical performances are totally satisfactory. But nothing can be done about it at this instant; the disapproving frown will avail nothing. Express your sincere appreciation; give real encouragement. Save your corrections for the next rehearsal.

PERFORMANCE IS THE ULTIMATE TEST OF THE MUSIC PROGRAM

Did We Say Anything Today?

While there may be significant side benefits, musical performance remains the principal product of the church music program (p. 27). If the public performance of the ensembles is not consistently good or excellent, something is amiss in the program.

It is perhaps impossible for the director of music to be completely objective in appraising the quality of his own work. Our ears are disposed to hear our own music as it ought to be rather than as it is. Deeply involved in the preparation of the music, we may unconsciously accept good intentions and honest effort as a substitute for superior results. With his customary candor, Father William Finn, one of the pioneers in the 20th century renascence of choral art, once observed that "The average choirmaster honestly misjudges the mediocrity of his own work."

However difficult, objective appraisal is nonetheless of supreme importance to the continued progress of your church music program. Each Sunday, after an anthem is completed, ask yourself the single most important question in church music: "Did we say anything today?" For, above all else, to succeed, music must communicate.

The Musical Pilgrim's Progress, a Lifelong Quest

Church music today offers one of the most stimulating challenges in the entire field of music. A useful choral ensemble can be organized in nearly any congregation: large or small, rich or poor, rural or urban. The opportunity and the ingredients are present nearly everywhere. What is most urgently needed is a catalyst to get things moving. In choral music, the only effective catalyst is the director. A capable and dedicated director can succeed almost anywhere by following the dictum of George Washington Carver: "Start where you are, with what you have, and make something of it ... "

Self-deception and self-satisfaction are the greatest obstacles to musical progress. When musical growth stops, musical decay sets in. No musician ever really "arrives"; excellence is literally a lifelong quest. Most symphonic conductors reach the apex of their careers at an age when other men have lapsed into a routine of sunshine, sand, and shuffleboard.

To pilgrims on the musical journey, each pinnacle attained is but a stepping-stone to a greater height; there is no turning back. Travel in the spirit of Pablo Casals, who observed, as he passed his eightieth birthday, "I study and practice each day, and continue to make some progress."

APPENDIX

Church Music for Every Occasion

According to my records, this is the music which my church choirs have sung most frequently or most effectively. Some are great, most are good, a few are mediocre. These latter would be replaced in the repertory if I knew of a better musical treatment of their useful texts.

The occasions at which the music has been sung are also indicated. This is, of course, quite arbitrary, and many of the selections would fit comfortably into worship services other than those indicated.

Dayton W. Nordin

*   *   *   *

Title	Composer	Publisher

Advent 1   Hosanna to the Son of David   Praetorius   S.H. McC.[1]
Bright, rhythmic, homophonic. SSATB a cap.
Lift Up Your Heads   Hammerschmidt   Willis
For larger chorus, predominately homophonic. SSATBB a cap.

Advent 2   Virga Jesse   A. Bruckner   Peters
One of the greatest motets ever written. SATB a cap.
Latin text only; print the translation in the bulletin.

Advent 3   Prepare Ye the Way of the Lord   W. James   Fitzsimons
Dramatic and forceful; needs big choir. SSATBB a cap.

Prepare the Way   Luvaas   Ditson
Effective setting of a great Swedish chorale. SATB, descant.

---

[1] Schmitt, Hall, and McCreary.

	Title	Composer	Publisher

Advent 4 Watchman Tell Us of the Night   Hovhaness   Peters
Classic form, contemporary harmonies. SATB, organ.

My Song in the Night   P. Christiansen   S.H. McC.
Southern Folk Hymn; beautiful. SATB a cap., opt. sop. solo.

Only Begotten Word   J.H. Wood   Concordia
Based on 9th cent. plainsong. SATB, organ, brass choir optional.

Rise, Arise   P. Norman   Kjos
Sturdy SATB chorale arr.; a perennial favorite.

General Advent   The Angel's Greeting   Brahms   Kjos
From the Marienleider, somewhat condensed. SATB a cap.

Gabriel's Message   Schalk   Concordia
Delightful arr. of Basque carol. SATB, a cap., sop. solo.

O Jesus, Grant Me Hope and Comfort   Franck   S.H. McC.
Pleasing, sentimental music. SATB, some male divisi, a cap.

Christmas   A Child Is Born in Bethlehem   M. Pooler   Augsburg
A Danish carol; quiet, gentle. SATB a cap. Opt. solo.

A Glad Noel   W. Ehret   Concordia
Bright, lively French tune. SATB, piano, sop. solo.

The Angel's Song   H. Grieb   G. Schirmer
Gay and bouncy. SATB, keyboard.

Still, Still, Still   R. Wetzler   Augsburg
German folksong; quiet, charming. SATB, organ, opt. flute.

Stars of Ice   D. Walker   Concordia
Chinese Christmas Carol, unique text and melody.
2 voices, light percussion.

Jesus, Jesus, Rest Your Head   P. Christiansen   Art Masters
Tender Appalachian carol. SATB a cap., opt. solo.

Glory to God in the Highest   Pergolesi   G. Schirmer
SS duet, SATB chorus, organ. Still shines brightly.

While Shepherds Watched Their Sheep   Jungst   H.W. Gray
Put the echo choir at the rear of the church. SATB a cap.

Angels Hovered 'Round   P. Christiansen   S.H. McC.
Quiet, contemplative. Some Latin phrases. SSATB a cap.

Now the Holy Child Is Born   Kelley   Boston
Effective arr. of familiar French carol. SSATB a cap.

Glory Be to God in Heaven   Snow   Homeyer
Delightful version of a familiar Noel. SATB a cap.

Cherubim Song #7   Bortniansky   H.W. Gray
Capable of exquisite performance. SATB a cap.

Title	*Composer*	*Publisher*

To Us Is Born Immanuel   Praetorius   S.H. McC.
Skillfully voiced for antiphonal effect. SATB a cap.

Name of Jesus   The Name of Jesus   Des Pres   Concordia
Early polyphony in classic canon form. SATB a cap.

Epiphany   Star in the East   Boatwright   E.C. Schirmer
Ky. folkhymn; imaginative harmonization. SATB, a cap.
Optional solos for all voices.

Epiphany 1   Meditation   Brahms   S.H. McC.
Heber's hymn, "By Cool Siloam's Shady Rill," with a Brahms' folksong
melody. It works. SATB a cap.

Epiphany 2   Good News   J. Marshall   C. Fischer
Luke 4:16-19 SATB, organ, reader, bar. solo. Ends with congregational
hymn, AZMON. Slightly modern.

Epiphany 3   Come Down, Lord   Winter/Roff   Vanguard
Matt. 8:5-8 in folksong style. SATB, keyboard.

Epiphany 4   Fierce Was the Wild Billow   T.T. Noble   Gamble
Dramatic setting of St. Anatolius' hymn. SSATB, a cap.

Transfiguration   How Lovely Is Thy Dwellingplace   A. Bruckner   Fitzsimons
Beautifully structured music. Practical for any choir. SATB a cap.

Jesus, These Eyes Have Never Seen   W. Skeat   J. Fischer
Hymn well matched to a Cruger chorale melody. SATB, organ.

Feb. 2 Presentation   Presentation of Christ in the Temple   J. Eccard   G.
Schirmer
A classic motet by a master choral composer. SSATBB a cap.

Nunc Dimittis   Gretchaninov   Boston
Impressive Russian-style sonority. SATB, some divisi.

Nunc Dimittis   Arkhangelsky   S.H. McC.
Rhythmic, and Russian, not difficult. SATB a cap.

Septuagesima   Fight the Good Fight   Thiman   H.W. Gray
Sturdy, original hymn-tune. Unison, descant, organ.

Sexagesima   Fertile Ground   Landgrave   Broadman
Luke 8:4-15, the parable of the seeds in folk-hymn style. 2-part; piano,
other instruments ad lib.

Blessed Jesus, At Thy Word   J.S. Bach   Concordia
Moderately difficult for organist; instrumental part can also be played by
string trio. SATB.

Title	Composer	Publisher

Quinquagesima   Open Our Eyes   Macfarlane   G. Schirmer
Always effective if not overdramatized. SATB, bar. solo., a cap; some divisi.

But the Greatest of These Is Charity   Day   H. Flammer
A winsome presentation of this marvelous text. SATB, organ.

Ash Wednesday   When I Survey the Wondrous Cross   D. Williams   H.W. Gray
Watts' hymn is derived from the Ash Wednesday Epistle. Original hymn-tune in the Welsh idiom. SATB, organ.

Lent 1   Man Shall Not Live by Bread Alone   Gardner   H. Flammer
Serviceable music; the text keeps it in the repertory. Luke 4:1-4. SATB, organ, tenor and bass soli.

Jesus Walked This Lonesome Valley   Prentice   Sacred Songs
Tasteful arr. preserving the character of the original material. SATB, organ, flute, bells (vibes), snare drum, guitar, and bass.

Lent 2   Call to Remembrance   Farrant   Birchard
Polyphonic writing of classic simplicity and beauty. SATB a cap. Text is the Introit for the day.

Lent 3   Savior, Thy Dying Love   C. Black   J. Fischer
Hymn-anthem. SATB, organ, opt. solo, congregation on final stanza, with descant.

Lent 4   Seek Ye the Lord   Roberts   C. Fischer
A Victorian standard. Still effective with the right tenor soloist, SATB choir, organ.

Come to the Waters   Vittoria   Ricordi
While most of Vittoria's music is somber, this bubbles with joy! Latin and English (good). SATB a cap.

God's Son Has Made Me Free   Grieg/Overby   Augsburg
A simplified version that is more effective for church use than Grieg's original. SATB a cap.

Lent 5   Send Forth Thy Light   Balakirev/Cain   S.H. McC.
Psalm 43:3,5. Good dynamic contrasts. SATB a cap.

Lamb of God   F.M. Christiansen   Augsburg
Based on the Decius chorale; among the least pretentious yet most enduringly beautiful of Dr. Christiansen's arrangements. SATB a cap.

God So Loved the World   J. Stainer   G. Schirmer
With the Old Testament Lesson for the day, use the bass recitative which precedes this chorus in the "Crucifixion": "And as Moses lifted up the serpent . . . " SATB a cap.

	Title	Composer	Publisher

Palm Sunday Hosanna   Gregor/Bitgood   H.W. Gray
Unison (or 2-pt) choir and SATB, organ. Accentuate the antiphony by positioning the choirs well apart.

Christus Factus Est (English text)   A. Bruckner   Summy
SATB a cap; moderately difficult, but spine-tingling. The English version is a model of choral editing.

Holy Week In Gethsemane   A. Bruckner   S.H. McC.
Text from Mark 14:32-36. Intensely devotional. SATB a cap.

Surely He Hath Borne Our Griefs   Lotti   E.C. Schirmer
Rare combination of technical simplicity and artistic excellence. SA(T)B a cap.

Surely He Bore Our Sorrows   Vittoria   E. Schirmer
More dramatic and more difficult than the Lotti above. Vittoria at his best. SATB a cap, good English text.

Lent, General Amazing Grace   J. Coates   Shawnee
Outstanding for the tasteful use of pop-Gospel piano accompaniment. SATB.

Behold the Lord's Hand   Van Hulse   Fitzsimons
Deeply penetential, quietly dramatic. SATB a cap.

Daughters of Zion   Mendelssohn   Boosey
From his unfinished oratorio,"Christus." SATB, organ

Go to Dark Gethsemane   T.T. Noble   H.W. Gray
Powerful setting of the great Lenten hymn. SATB, a cap, some divisi.

Incline Thine Ear   Arkhangelsky   Witmark
Excellent English text; skillfully voiced. SATB a cap.

Hide Not Thou Thy Face   Farrant   E.C. Schirmer
Prayer, beautifully expressed in music. SATB, a cap.

Lord, for Thy Tender Mercies' Sake   Farrant   E.C. Schirmer
Quiet, deeply devotional. SATB a cap.

O Saviour of the World   J. Goss   G. Schirmer
Survives from Victorian times because it has something to say, and says it very well. SATB, organ ad lib.

Easter Ye Sons and Daughters of the King   Leisring   E.C. Schirmer
Antiphonal SATB & TTBB. Rhythmically exciting, with the marvelous choral sonority of the early homophonic works.

This Is the Day   Gallus   Concordia
Very festive double chorus: SATB & SATB. Chorus II may be replaced by brass qtte. Parts provided.

Jesus Christ Is Risen Today   Hovhaness   Associated
Masterful use of traditional, contemporary and Oriental music principles.

Title	*Composer*	*Publisher*

Novel and exciting. SATB, 2 keyboard instruments, and tamtam.

Today Did Christ Arise   Whitehead   Ditson
17th Century Dutch Carol; the upsurging melodic line especially appropriate to Easter theme. SATB a cap.

Easter 1   Magdelena (from the Marienlieder)   Brahms   G. Schirmer
German and very good English texts. Beautiful Brahms, and not at all difficult. SATB a cap.

Easter 2   (The following might also be appropriate for Trinity 3)
A Faithful Shepherd Is My God   Nageli/Stein   S.H. McC.
Paraphrase Psalm 23; 6/8 pastorale. Pleases many. SATB a cap.

Psalm 23   Zimmerman   Augsburg
Chant-like melodic line; organ part based on St. Columba. SATB, organ, double bass. Fresh and utterly charming.

My Shepherd Will Supply My Need   V. Thompson   H.W. Gray
Another paraphrase of Ps. 23; old Southern hymn tune. Arranged by a master musician. SATB a cap.

All in the April Evening   Roberton   G. Schirmer
The smooth homophony well-suited to the sentimental text. SATB a cap.

Brother James' Air   Jacobs   C. Fischer
Yet another paraphrase of Ps. 23; folk-type tune. SATB a cap.

Easter 4   O Sing to the Lord a New Song   Prentice   Sacred Songs
From a cantata: The Day of Resurrection. SATB, 8-horn brass choir, tympani and percussion. Contemporary techniques employed with great expressive power. Requires full resources.

Ascension   O Spotless Lamb   Bach/Thoburn   Augsburg
Beautiful Bach, practical for any choir. SATB a cap.

If Ye Love Me, Keep My Commandments   Tallis   Summy
Beloved by the admirers of Tudor music. SATB a cap.

Crown Him with Many Crowns   Pelz   Augsburg
When you need a post-Easter lift. Concertato on the familiar hymn. SATB, descant, congregation, 3 trumpets, organ.

Easter, General   Christ Our Lord, Who Died to Save Us   Praetorius   Concordia
Unique conception for four SATB choirs (small o.k.) each accompanied by a different family of instruments: strings, recorders (flutes), winds. Parts provided. The hardest part is getting organized; performance is easy.

Still with Thee   M. Pooler   Augsburg
A sensitive setting of Ps. 139:9,10,18b. SATB a cap.

Confirmation   Lord, Sanctify Me Wholly   Pasquet   Fitzsimons
Thomas Ken's prayer, easy and imaginatively set. SATB a cap.

Title	*Composer*	*Publisher*

Thine Forever, God of Love   Roff   Concordia
Smooth chorale melody, traditional harmonies. SATB a cap.

Pentecost   Emitte Spiritum Tuum   Schuetky   J. Fischer
Deservedly one of the most popular of motets. Many editions; this has Latin and English. SSATTBB a cap.

Let Thy Blessed Spirit   Tschesnokoff   J. Fischer
Classic Russian choral writing. Interesting voicings. SSATTBB a cap.

Come Holy Ghost   Palestrina   G. Schirmer
Appropriate text for Palestrina's hymn-tune. This version somewhat over-edited. SATB a cap.

Trinity Sunday   Credo   Gretchaninov   Boston
Marvelous if you have the right alto soloist, and the absolutely essential deep bass voices in the chorus. SSAATTBB a cap. English text.

Hymn to the Trinity   Tschaikovsky   H.W. Gray
Verse-refrain format; good text, beautifully constructed music. SATB a cap.

Trinity 1   O Thou in Whom We Live and Move   Bach/Malin   Birchard
Samuel Longfellow's poem teamed with a Bach chorale arrangement. SATB a cap.

Trinity 2   The Wedding Banquet   Winter/Roff   Vanguard
The famed parable in folk-hymn style. Lively and appealing. SATB, piano pref.

God Be in My Head   Davies   H.W. Gray
Words from a children's primer of 1558. Conventional but satisfying music. SATB a cap, occasional divisi.

Trinity 3   Cast Thy Burden Upon the Lord   Mendelssohn   G. Schirmer
SATB, occasional arpeggios: piano? harp? Vibraharp?

For Trinity 3, see also listing for Easter 2

Trinity 5   He Comes to Us   J. Marshall   C. Fischer
A very effective anthem, text from a theological summation by Albert Schweitzer. "Wie Schoen," as a concluding chorale, is optional. SATB, keyboard.

Trinity 14   How Lovely Is Thy Dwellingplace   Bruckner   Fitzsimons
Text is the Introit for the day, in a setting of ethereal beauty. SATB a cap.

Ten Lepers   Winter/Roff   Vanguard
The Gospel parable in popular folk hymn style. SATB, piano pref.

Trinity 17   Wherewith Shall I Come Before the Lord?   Bush   J. Church
A most thought-provoking text; well-crafted setting; SATB a cap.

Title	Composer	Publisher

Trinity 21   For the Living of These Days   D. Blakley   Broadman
  A "production" for SATB, brass qtte., tympani, organ, minister and congregation. Exciting and satisfying participation.

Trinity 25   At the River   A. Copland   Boosey
  The old-time Gospel hymn with contemporary touches. SATB, piano.

All Saints'   Sing Ye Righteous   Viadana   Concordia
  A favorite motet with the Sistine Chapel choir. Psalm 33:1-3. Latin and English. SATB a cap.
  In Heaven Above   Grieg   Peters
  The great Norwegian hymn; beautiful beyond words with a good soloist and well-tuned choir. SATB a cap., bar. solo.

  In Heaven Above   F.M. Christiansen   Augsburg
  Format similar to the Grieg version, but easier. SATB, solo, a cap.

  The Beatitudes   H.R. Evans   Remick
  Still a very useful setting. SATB, bar. solo, organ.

  For All the Saints   R. Johnston   Shawnee
  The famed Mormon hymn. SATB, some divisi. You may be tempted to re-edit a few spots, but it's very effective.

Thanksgiving   Sing to the Lord of Harvest   H. Willan   Concordia
  An English Harvest hymn, a lively German tune, and a master musician to arrange the marriage. SATB, organ.

Praise; Loud or Lively   O Lord, Thou Art My God and King   Sateren
  Augsburg
  Paraphrase of Ps. 145; traditional Scotch tune. SATB a cap.

  Variants for "St. Anne"   Coke-Jephcott   H.W. Gray
  "O God, Our Help" in a stirring arrangement. SATB, organ, opt. 3 trumpets and tympani, can also add congregation.

  Sing Praise to God   Pfautsch   Summy
  "Mit Freuden Zart" arr. SATB, organ. Good voicing and rhythmic variety.

  Psalm 124   Parker-Shaw   Lawson-Gould
  Rugged metrical psalm from the Ainsworth Psalter. Of historical as well as musical interest. SATB a cap.

  God of Our Fathers   Gearhart   Shawnee
  Flashy, festival music. Familiar hymn for SATB, 2 keyboards, or full band accompaniment.

  Come, Thou Fount of Every Blessing   Pfautsch   Lawson-Gould
  Tune "Warrenton" in a buoyant arr. SATB a cap, some divisi.

  B'Shuv Adonai (Psalm 126)   Ades   Shawnee
  Traditional Hebrew melody; English and Hebrew texts. SATB, piano, tambourine, finger cymbals.

Title	*Composer*	*Publisher*

All Glory Be to God on High   Praetorius   Augsburg
Decius' chorale for two SATB choirs a cap. Choir I can be a qtte.

Quiet, Contemplative Wondrous Love   P. Christiansen   Augsburg
A deft touch with folksong material. SATB a cap., opt. solo.

There Is a Balm in Gilead   Howorth   Belwin
Interesting, but not overdone arr. SATB a cap., sop. solo.

See What Love Hath the Father Bestowed   Mendelssohn
G. Schirmer
From the oratorio "St. Paul." SATB, pref. a cap. Text is 1 John 3:1.

My God, How Wonderful Thou Art   Overby   Augsburg
Tune "Dundee" from Scottish Psalter; hymn by Faber. SATB a cap, sop.
solo.

I Will Lift Up Mine Eyes (Ps.121:1-4)   Dvorak   C. Fischer
Quiet, introspective, lyric. SATB, keyboard, mezzo solo.

I Waited for the Lord   Mendelssohn   G. Schirmer
S-S duet, SATB chorus, keyboard. From "Hymn of Praise."

I Heard a Voice from Heaven   Goss   E.C. Schirmer
Rev 14:13, words and music of great comfort. SATB a cap.

Choral Prayer   O Thou the True and Only Light   Mendelssohn   Birchard
Chorale from "St. Paul." SATB, organ.

Support Us, Lord   H. Morgan   J. Fischer
One of the most beautiful prayers in the English language. Homophonic,
SATB, a cap.

Prayer for Peace   P. Fetler   Augsburg
Deeply devotional, with a touch of modern harmony. SATB a cap.

Only Begotten Word of God Eternal   Brown   H.W. Gray
Medieval melody skillfully arranged. SATB, opt. solo, organ.

Lead Me, Lord   S.S. Wesley   G. Schirmer
A gem that has not lost its luster. SATB, organ, opt. mezzo solo.

Lead Me, O Father   Bach/Luvaas   Volkwein
Useful text, masterful chorale harmonization. SATB a cap.

Hear My Prayer   Arcedelt   E.C. Schirmer
A classic of religious song; early homophony. SATB a cap.

Communion   O Bread of Life   F.M. Christiansen   Augsburg
The Isaak chorale imaginatively voiced. SATB, bar. solo, a cap.

Let All Mortal Flesh Keep Silence   G. Holst   Galaxy
Tune "Picardy." Sop. and bar. soli. SATB, organ, some divisi. Orchestra
parts on rental. Builds to spine-tingling climax.

Jesus, Word of God Incarnate   Mozart   Ditson
English version of the famous Ave Verum. SATB, organ.

Remember Our Savior   Eberlin   S.H. McC.

Title	*Composer*	*Publisher*

Early 18th Century motet. Latin and Eberlin English text. Attractive voicing and Mozart-style harmonies. SATB a cap.

Of the Glorious Body Telling   Vittoria   Augsburg
The translation of Thomas Aquinas' poem is acceptable, but it is Vittoria's transcendent music that keeps this in the repertory. SATB a cap.

I Am the Bread of Life   Stainer   Belwin
John 5:33, dramatized in Victorian style, but not overdone. SATB, organ, opt. solo.

O Hidden Savior   Gregorian/Sateren   Augsburg
Haunting plainsong melody in soprano, ATB humming accomp. English text.

Longer Works

Liturgical Music   Misa Criolla   Ramirez   Lawson-Gould
Folk Mass based on Spanish-American melodies and rhythms. Spanish and English texts. Two soloists, sopranos or high tenors, SATB chorus. Multiple percussion, guitar, harpsichord (piano). Novel and appealing, but reverent. About 30 minutes.

Mass for Joy   Peloquin   GIA Publications
English text, contemporary sound with jazz touches. Many voicings available, for congregation and choir, or choir alone. Flexible accompaniment: organ alone, or with guitars and bass. Concert version with brass choir and tympani. Well-received, even in traditional liturgical circles. Concert version about 12 minutes.

Gloria   Vivaldi   Franco-Colombo
Latin and English text. Soprano and mezzo solos, SATB chorus. Orchestration available on rental from the publisher. Can be done on keyboards, but less effective. Bright, lively Baroque music, steadily gaining in popularity. About 30 minutes.

Cantatas   Wake, Awake   Buxtehude   Augsburg
Three stanzas of "Wachet Auf": 1. Treble solo or unison. 2. Male solo or unison. 3. SAB chorus. Accompaniment: four violins and continuo. Nonpedantic Buxtehude, excellent for Advent. About 7 minutes.

Therefore Watch That Ye Be Ready   Hammerschmidt   Concordia
Bass solo (or section), SSATB chorus. Two violins, cello, keyboard. Based on the other great Nicolai chorale, "Wie Schön Leuchtet." German and excellent English text, especially for the Last Sunday in Trinity, incorporating a portion of the Gospel for that day, Matt. 24:44. About 7 minutes. A work of exceptional merit.

Woman, Why Weepest Thou?   Schutz   Concordia
The Easter dialogue of Jesus and Mary Magdelena (John 20:13-17). SATB soloists, or sections. Final chorus SSATB. Organ accompaniment. A beautiful and moving work. About 8 minutes.

Title	*Composer*	*Publisher*

O Holy Jesus   Rohlig   Concordia
Crueger's great passion chorale, "Herzliebster Jesu" in contemporary harmonizations. Cantor (reader), SATB chorus, optional soprano solo (section). Flute and organ accompaniment. About 12 minutes.

The Day of Resurrection   Prentice   Sacred Songs
Combines traditional, contemporary and avant-garde choral techniques to recreate in the service some of the genuine excitement and wonder of the first Easter Day. SATB chorus, full bass choir, tympani and multiple percussion. Two readers, and congregational participation. 18 unforgettable minutes.

God's Time Is the Best   J.S. Bach   Many editions
One of the finest of Bach cantatas for church use. A superior, Biblical text; although, you may not be pleased with all of the available translations. SATB chorus and SATB soloists. Unusual orchestration: 2 recorders (flutes), viola, 2 celli, bass, keyboard. About 20 minutes.

Double Choirs   What Can Life Be but a Shadow?   Bach   G. Schirmer
Solemn, but comforting message; German and English. Largely homophonic, and sonorous; not typical Bach. SSATTB and ATB choirs, the latter can be much smaller than Choir I. About 6 minutes.

Sing to the Lord   Schutz   Kjos
Bright and lively, very much in the style of Schutz' teacher, Gabrieli. Text from Psalm 100, English. Two SATB choirs. About 4 minutes.

Concertatos   Built on a Rock   Bunjes   Concordia
Seven stanzas of the Lindeman chorale. SATB chorus, congregation, organ, trumpets. About 10 minutes.

Praise to the Lord   Rohlig   Concordia
"Lobe Den Herren" for SATB chorus, congregation, optional children's choir, flute, trumpet, organ. About 8 minutes.

I Know That My Redeemer Lives   Bunjes   Concordia
"Duke Street," 8 stanzas in varied voicings. SATB chorus, congregation, trumpet, organ. About 7 minutes.

Passions   Passion According to St. Matthew   Vittoria   Summy
Multiple readers, SATB chorus, a cappella. Chorus is the "turba." Homophonic in style, not difficult. About 21 minutes.

The Seven Words from the Cross   Nystedt   Augsburg
Bitter-sweet motifs and harmonizations beautifully portray the mood of Good Friday. Incorporates the Decius chorale, Lamb of God, most effectively. SATB, some divisi, cantor (reader), preferably a cappella. An unexcelled setting of the Seven Words for worship services. About 17 minutes.

Index